Team Code of Honor

The Secrets of Champions in Business and in Life

BLAIR SINGER

Team Code
of Honor

*The Secrets of Champions
in Business and in Life*

BLAIR SINGER

BZK PRESS

Published by BZK Press, LLC

Rich Dad Advisors, B-I Triangle, CASHFLOW Quadrant and other Rich Dad marks are registered trademarks of CASHFLOW Technologies, Inc.

BZK Press LLC
2248 Meridian Blvd.
Suite H
Minden, NV 89423
775-782-2201

Visit our Web sites: BZKPress.com MyBestAdvisors.com

Printed in the United States of America

First Edition: September 2004
First BZK Press Edition: June 2012

ISBN: 978-1-937832-12-4

Best-Selling Books
In the Rich Dad Advisors Series

by Blair Singer

SalesDogs
You Don't Have to Be an Attack Dog to Explode Your Income

Team Code of Honor
The Secrets of Champions in Business and in Life

by Garrett Sutton, Esq.

Start Your Own Corporation
Why the Rich Own Their Own Companies and Everyone Else Works for Them

Writing Winning Business Plans
*How to Prepare a Business Plan that Investors will Want to Read —
and Invest In*

Buying and Selling a Business
How You Can Win in the Business Quadrant

The ABCs of Getting Out of Debt
Turn Bad Debt into Good Debt and Bad Credit into Good Credit

Run Your Own Corporation
*How to Legally Operate and Properly Maintain Your Company
into the Future*

The Loopholes of Real Estate
Secrets of Successful Real Estate Investing

by Ken McElroy

The ABCs of Real Estate Investing
The Secrets of Finding Hidden Profits Most Investors Miss

The ABCs of Property Management
What You Need to Know to Maximize Your Money Now

The Advanced Guide to Real Estate Investing
How to Identify the Hottest Markets and Secure the Best Deals

by Tom Wheelwright

Tax-Free Wealth
How to Build Massive Wealth by Permanently Lowering Your Taxes

Acknowledgments and Dedication

This message has been inside me ever since the days I watched my father take on what seemed to me to be the monumental task of running a five-hundred-acre working dairy farm in northeastern Ohio. Coordinating the efforts of vendors, hired part-time help, laborers, our family and even the menagerie of animals was an act of leadership that could be decimated at any moment with a simple change in the weather.

As an avid football fan and head manager for the Ohio State football team under Woodrow Wayne Hayes, I learned powerful lessons on how to lead and drive great teams. That football program has been an inspiration in many ways throughout my life. I have been blessed to work with great coaches, great teams and powerful organizations over the years.

Specifically I want to thank Buckminster Fuller for showing me the reasons "why" I do what I do. To my family and grandparents for showing me what a real Code of Honor is. To my father and mother, for whom this subject is a passion to which both have committed a deep part of their lives. To my incredible loving wife, who was the first to teach me the true meaning of the word "trust." To my dear friend Robert Kiyosaki, who never fails to push me to be the person I dream to be. To Kim Kiyosaki for being an incredibly intense and competitive teammate and true friend.. To the whole Rich Dad team, which has been one of the greatest business teams I have been honored to be a part of. To Lee Somers, my cross-country coach in high school, who gave me my first taste of leadership, grit and endurance. To the warehouse team of my old air freight company, who taught me the true meaning of living by the code in the toughest of times and how love, work and discipline can make miracles happen.

Most important:

The message of this book is timeless. None of it is original. It is the stuff of great institutions, great nations, great families and great people. I owe any inspiration in this book to all of those throughout time who gave their lives, fortunes and spirits for ideals that would make all of our lives better. I want to thank all of those who in their own way lead us every day.

To those who have made mistakes and owned up to them. To those who try and fail and try again. To every kid who ever raised his or her hand with excitement to be part of the team. To those who tried out for the team and didn't make it but found their own teams to win on.

Most of all I dedicate this book to my two sons. If we can get them to realize and deliver their true gifts, they will touch thousands.

This is also dedicated to you. Everything you do makes a difference.

Blair Singer

Contents

Foreword
by Robert Kiyosaki

The Four Most Important Business Skills an Entrepreneur Must Have

There are many people who have a million-dollar idea for a product, yet they never turn their ideas into money. There are also millions of people who would love to quit their job and start their own business, yet their dream of being a business owner remains only a dream. Instead they choose to cling to a secure job. And of the people who do take the plunge and start their own business, many soon fail. Statistics show that 90 percent of all new businesses fail in the first five years—and that 90 percent of the 10 percent that do survive the first five years fail before the tenth year. Why?

Many experts say that people fail to start their own businesses, or fail soon after starting, due to two primary reasons. The reasons are a lack of money and a lack of business skills. Of the two, I would say that the lack of business skills is the most important. In other words, if you have the business skills, you can create the money. But if you have money and no business skills, the money is soon gone.

When my rich dad was training me to be an entrepreneur, he often said, "There are four main skills an entrepreneur must have or learn. They are *sales, accounting, investing,* and *leadership.*" He also said, "If an entrepreneur is struggling, it is often because he is weak in one or more of these business skills."

The books I write focus on two of these important business skills. They are *accounting* and *investing*. Most of us know of business people who have failed or struggled financially because their financial statements were not in order, or they squandered their money, failing to invest and reinvest their profits.

Blair Singer is a valued Rich Dad Advisor because he teaches some of the most essential skills for entrepreneurs: Sales, team building and leadership. His first Rich Dad Advisor book, *Sales Dogs,* is a must read for anyone who is or plans on being an entrepreneur. In my opinion, the ability to sell is the most important of the four business skills. I have met so many people who have great ideas but are unable to sell their ideas or their products. Without sales, there is no need for the other three skills— because there is no opportunity to use them.

The second vital skill Blair Singer is world famous for is his knowledge of team building and leadership training. One of the reasons my rich dad was glad I spent four years at a military academy and six years in the Marine Corps was for the leadership training. One of the reasons many entrepreneurs fail is simply that they lack the ability to build a team that will do the impossible to make their business a success.

In this book, you will learn about the Code of Honor. In my opinion, as a Marine Corps officer and pilot, it was the *code of honor* that gave my men and me the courage to operate as a unified team, overcome our own fears, and perform tasks that seemed impossible. Today, in my own businesses, it is this same *code of honor* that is core to much of my business and financial success.

The ability to lead and manage people is a vital business skill. In my opinion, one of the reasons many small businesses fail to grow or simply fail is that the entrepreneur does not put together a strong team and often quits the business out of exhaustion. My rich dad often said, "Getting people to operate as a team and do what you need them to do is the toughest task of any business owner." He also said, "Business is easy. Managing people is hard."

Read this book and find out how you can build a powerful business team that operates as a team and gets stronger even though the challenges get taller.

From another perspective: Lately, there has been much ado about the loss of jobs to countries such as China, Vietnam, and India. Today, even Mexico is losing jobs to these countries. The problem is so bad that many politicians promise that they will create jobs or punish companies that export jobs. Thankfully, most of us know that politicians' promises are often only promises, not to be kept.

Recently, on a trip to China, I learned that China has a larger unemployment problem than the West. I was told that every year in China, 18 million highly educated students graduate and enter the work force looking for a job. The same is happening in India, Pakistan, the Philippines, and other countries.

One of the reasons that job losses in the West will continue is that there are hundreds of millions of people in the world who are willing to work for four dollars a day. With transportation, communication, and technology costs going down, the idea of a secure, high-paying job with benefits is rapidly becoming a thing of the past. Promise as much as they like, no politician can stop this global development.

Today, in spite of this global trend of job competition, students still go to school so they can find a secure job once they graduate. Talk about an obsolete idea. One of the reasons this book is so important is that today, the world needs more entrepreneurs, people who can build businesses and *create* jobs, rather than people who *need* jobs.

Robert Kiyosaki

Introduction

The Code of Honor

On January 3, 2003, the Ohio State University football team met the defending national champion Miami Hurricanes in the Fiesta Bowl to determine a new national champion, in what became, according to sports analysts, one of the most exciting games in the history of college football. And while this introductory story is about two specific football teams, it could be about any two teams in sports. It could be the Boston Red Sox in the ninth inning of the fourth game of the 2004 American League Championship Series in which, being down three games to none to the New York Yankees, embarked on an unprecedented comeback to defeat the Yankees in the series and go on to win the World Series of baseball.

It could be the 1983 Australian America's Cup yacht racing team, down three races to one in the best of seven races as they stormed back to beat the undefeated Americans by a margin of only forty-two seconds over six days of racing.

It could be the group of amateur hockey players that comprised the U.S. Olympic Hockey team that went on to beat the heavily favored world champion Soviet team in the 1980 Winter Olympics and ultimately win the Gold medal.

It could be the design and marketing teams of Apple computer as they began their battle back from the brink of extinction in 1997 with Steve Jobs at the helm in one of the biggest business comebacks in recent history.

It could be you and your business team breaking into a new line of business....Your family facing the obstacles of a tough economy...

As a spectator at the game that I began to describe earlier, and as a former student manager for the Ohio State team, I could not help but get caught up in the tension and excitement of the game. Yet beyond the game itself, there was a very powerful lesson. There is one thing that the winners in each of these situations have in common as you shall see.

Let me describe the scene briefly.

Two great teams had taken to the playing field. The energy was incredibly high. The prognosticators had made their predictions. The crowd was on the edge of their seats. For weeks every fan had known that the season was leading up to this clash of titans.

The talent on both sides of the field was impressive. The strategies, tactics and game plans were simple but powerful. From the very beginning of the game, each player seemed to play to his fullest potential. Each team made mistakes but neither team was fazed by them. The game ebbed and flowed, and with each passing moment, the crowd's excitement built higher and higher.

For the players, fatigue seemed to disappear as the game wore on. No one panicked. No one broke ranks. The years of practice, discipline and focus came down to the waning minutes of the game. Who was going to win? The favored defending champions? Or the scrappy underdogs?

The teams battled to a tie. The game went into overtime. Both of them scored. It then went into a second overtime. The fans were now going wild. It seemed that these two undefeated teams had met on the playing field to see which was the team of "destiny."

In watching this game as a spectator, I began to smile. The longer the game wore on, the more certain I became about the outcome. Why? Because in my years of working with great teams I have found that the great champions in sports, business and families have one thing in common. It is legitimately their secret weapon.

It isn't a strategy. It isn't a plan. It isn't technology. It isn't a trick play or twist on an old theme. And it definitely is not luck! It is something that lies deep in the genetic code of winning organizations. It is something so ingrained in the hearts and spirits of the players that it is sometimes unconscious. Yet its presence is undeniable.

It's something that shows its face when the pressure is high, when the stakes are critical and when everything is on the line. You see it in families when there is a crisis. You'll find it in businesses when the cash runs tight. It shows up in each of us when we are put to the test of having to deliver or falter. It's called the Code of Honor.

In the waning moments of that second overtime, the undefeated defending national champions were positioned inside the ten yard line with four downs to score a touchdown. Ohio State, a fifteen-point underdog, was faced with having to defend against the most powerful team in college football.

Two teams of destiny. Which would win? Almost as if by magic, Ohio State successfully kept Miami out of the end zone each successive down. The crowd was out of its mind. The noise was deafening. Yet when the smoke cleared, Ohio State had held on and won the national championship.

Was it luck? Was it talent? Was it strategy? I have always been intrigued by how teams in sports emerge as winners even against the odds. I have always pondered how a person who has little talent and few resources can become rich. How does a floundering business all of a sudden shoot to success from obscurity?

I found that it is the same thing that holds families together under pressure. It is a tool that is common with all great teams. It is the Code of Honor.

It is a set of simple, powerful rules that govern the internal behavior of any team, organization, family, individual and even nation. These rules determine how we behave toward one another within the team. They are its heart and spirit. They are what people are willing to stand and defend— and be accountable for.

They're rules like never abandoning a teammate in need, and being personally responsible for all mistakes. Yet what I'm talking about goes even beyond rules, because many teams have rules. It is the unwavering discipline of the team itself to enforce those rules. Not to rely on bosses, coaches, regulators, parents or ministers to enforce them, but to have the team spontaneously support each other in adhering to the code. It's repeated, practiced and drilled so many times in so many instances that it becomes unconsciously embedded in the hearts of the players. The code builds trust, cohesion and energy.

In building a championship team in your business, in your family or in your group, there is a difference between good and great. It's the invisible magic that shows up when pressure is high and challenges seem insurmountable. That magic is the Code of Honor. It pervades every part of the team, every statement, every action, every heartbeat. It is a statement of who you are and what you stand for.

It's more than values. It is your values extended into real, physical behavior. These are the rules that set the standards of conduct and performance.

The good news is that you can create this code for yourself and your team. It is Rich Dad's secret for building great teams. No matter where you go or what you do it will be present. If you know how to build it, maintain it and protect it, you will attract only the best players and you will experience the repeated magic of championship results whether it's in the arena of money, health or even love.

In Robert Kiyosaki's *CASHFLOW Quadrant,* he talks at great length about the differences in attitude, mindset and behavior of folks in the B-business quadrant as opposed to the E-employee and S-self-employed quadrants. The number-one skill in business is the ability to sell. In the book *SalesDogs,* we demystified this issue about negotiating and communicating for what you want. Everyone sells in every area of life whether you are in direct selling or not. It's Rich Dad's number-one skill.

But as important as the ability to sell, what distinguishes business owners from self-employed folks is their ability to build a great team. As a practitioner, service provider or one-man band that trades time for money, you work hard, but have little leverage. Those who understand the secrets found in this book will catapult their way to wealth in the B quadrant by learning how to surround themselves with the right people and how to ensure that they are on the same track. Building teams is not "happy camp" and it's not what we have been trained to do most of our lives. For some it comes easily. For others, it takes challenging yourself and your beliefs about others, and a clear understanding of the Code of Honor.

It's not rocket science, but it requires a test of will. This book will walk you through the process so that you can create championship results any time and in any place.

Ohio State won the game with a great team. Yet the difference between the two teams became revealed in the moments of challenge. It was the set of rules that they had long before adopted that set the standards of performance. The rules of the winning team instilled a confidence, discipline and magic that under pressure made them calmer, more focused and ultimately, winners. Each team had a code, knowingly or not. But the rules in those codes were different.

You will learn how to spot those differences and correct them.

In nearly every interview in which the players of championship teams are questioned about the motivation that inspired them to win, no matter what country, what sport, what language, they say the same thing. When coaches and players are asked, they all say that *they played the game for each other, for their teammates.* It was not about stardom, not about beating the other team. It was about supporting each other. That comes from a very specific type of Code!

John Bertrand, the 1983 America's Cup winning Australian skipper, summed it up well. He said, "The Americans had a team of champions, but we were a Championship Team." They had a powerful code and set of rules that were significantly different from those of the American team.

How all these teams pulled together to win is what you will learn by the time you finish this book.

This book is dedicated to you having all the championship teams in your life that you so richly deserve. It is your right to be happy, to be rich, and to surround yourself with great players who share your vision and spirit.

WHY the Code?

I speak all over the world and have worked with thousands of teams and hundreds of thousands of individuals, helping them increase their incomes through sales and team building. Everyone seems to want a "silver bullet" solution that will attract the best players and produce extraordinary results from their teams. Parents seem to want some magic answer to managing their kids and handling their households.

There have been thousands of books written on teams, peak performance, child-rearing and how to get rich. And most of them repeat similar principles and lessons. Yet most of them ignore this incredibly powerful component. The idea of a Code of Honor isn't a new one. It's always been there. But like most things, we take it for granted until something bad happens.

Throughout the 1990s it seemed that everyone was on the path to learning how to get rich quickly. If you invested in an Internet business you were considered a genius.

Yet in the spring of 2001, the beginning of a major shift in how we all looked at business, and life, started to take place. The dotcom bubble popped. Markets took a dive. We all kind of took a blow to the chin. Business owners and individuals started reassessing their priorities when it came to spending and investing. With pressure to show profits, some turned to alternative and questionable means for reporting their results in order to continue to attract investment funds.

Then, on September 11, we took a major blow to the midsection. The greatest and most horrific act of terrorism we have ever known was played out before our eyes, over and over again. With the terrible events that day, priorities took an even bigger shift.

Until that awful morning, we thought we were invincible. We thought nothing could touch us. But we were wrong. It came to many of us in a flash that nothing was safe—not our offices, not our government, not our airplanes, not even our mail. It was time to get serious about what *really* mattered in life, because it was actually possible that we might not have tomorrow. It wasn't just about how much money we made, it was about the people in our lives and assessing what was *really* important.

Corporate scandals, one after the other, eroded our hope that the people we worked for, or invested money with, could be trusted. The list of questionable business practices, like those in Enron, WorldCom or even revered institutions like Arthur Anderson, just kept growing. Now we wonder, where is *their* Code of Honor? It has become painfully clear that either none existed, or nobody enforced it, or it was not a Code of Honor but a code of deceit.

My point is this: In the absence of rules, people make up their own.

Those differences can become catastrophic in the heat of the battle, particularly where stress is high and confusion is prevalent. Those who are successful have a very clear Code of Honor that is easy to understand and is not negotiable or subject to multiple interpretations. It's a strong set of rules that everyone around them agrees to and it's part of what makes everyone around them successful as well.

But it's not enough to just *have* a code. If all the players on a team don't know the rules or don't interpret them in the same way, the team can't win. The players on your team have to understand the code, and commit themselves to respecting it.

The heart and soul of every team is its Code of Honor. Rules like being on time, practicing, showing up, attending training sessions, committing to personal growth or never abandoning a teammate in need. These rules not only ensure success, they make the game a lot more satisfying to play. Great relationships don't happen by accident. There is usually a common understanding and set of rules holding you together.

A Code of Honor is the cornerstone of the culture of any organization because it is the physical manifestation of its thoughts, ideals and philosophies. People talk about creating culture in organizations. I have been part of several large culture creations, revitalizations and change initiatives with clients. The core of the culture and the number-one tool used to establish, refresh, broadcast and demonstrate the culture is the Code of Honor.

Developing a Code of Honor creates accountability and a feeling of support and is a powerful statement of who you are and what your team stands for. It defines you and your goals. It's that important.

So how do you develop a Code of Honor that all team players will respect and adhere to, whether it's in your business, your family or your community? That's what you're about to find out.

Team Tips:

- In the absence of rules, people make up their own.

- Successful people and groups have a very clear Code of Honor that is easy to understand and is not negotiable.

- Developing a Code of Honor creates accountability and a feeling of support and is a powerful statement of who you are and what your team stands for.

Team Drill:

1. Discuss with your team examples of close games, great comebacks and championship results in sports and business. Talk about what you think made the difference, beyond talent.

2. Cite examples of organizations that had rules but didn't follow them. Have the team discuss their opinions of those organizations.

Chapter One

Why Do You Need a Code of Honor?

In the absence of rules, people make up their own rules. And some of the biggest collisions in finance, business and relationships occur because well-meaning people are simply playing by different sets of rules. By the same token, the most miraculous results come from "like-minded" folks who band together under some invisible bond to achieve greatness.

By experience and default, we all formulate our own sets of guidelines, rules and assumptions. That's natural. But when we start coming together with other people, organizations and cultures, we sometimes have a tough time figuring out why "those guys" don't understand, or how they could so blatantly turn their back on our feelings, our way of doing things and our rules. In most respects, "those guys" feel the same way about us. Why? Because we assume that certain basic rules are the same. Bad assumption.

This book is about revealing the process for eliminating one of the biggest causes for financial loss, frustration and heartbreak. It is about surrounding yourself with folks who subscribe to the same sets of rules and how to establish them so that you can ensure peak performance, fun and incredible results in all you do.

For about twelve years now, I've actively studied teams; looking at what makes them successful and how they are able to operate at peak performance. And after all this time, I can tell you this: You cannot have a championship team, in any facet of your life, without a Code of Honor.

Team Tip:

Sometimes the easiest way to avoid upset, collisions and disharmony in any group is to take the time to make sure that everyone is playing by the same rules.

If you are interested in building a great relationship, whether it's with your business, your community, your family or even yourself, there have to be rules and standards for the behavior that will ultimately achieve your goals. A Code of Honor is the physical manifestation of the team's values, extended into behavior. It's not enough to *have* values, because we all do. What's so crucial is knowing how to put physical behavior into practice to reflect those values.

Let me illustrate what I mean. When I was in high school in Ohio, I was on the cross-country running team. Typically, any human being of the male sex living in the state of Ohio was expected to play football. But if you could see my size, you'd realize that I was just not built to go up against a two-hundred-pound linebacker, even though I love the game. Cross-country was more my style.

What a lot of people don't know about cross-country is that there are typically about five to seven runners per team racing at the same time. Usually there are several other teams running at the same time. The only way your team can win is if the whole team finishes relatively close together close to the front of the pack of runners. In other words, having a superstar who runs ahead of the pack and places first doesn't do the team any good if everyone else is all spread out across the field. Cross-country is a low-scoring sport, meaning that first place receives a point, second receives two points, and so on. The idea is to get the whole team to finish near the front, so your team gets the lowest score possible. If we could get fourth-, sixth-, seventh- and ninth-place finishes, then even if another team got a first, second, twelfth and eighteenth, we would still win the meet.

So for the entire two-and-a-half-mile race each of us would push the others on, encouraging, threatening, supporting, and yelling with each gasping breath for air. With muscles burning and body strength faltering, it was as much a race of emotional endurance as it was physical. We pushed each other both on and off the course. If someone was slacking, you can rest assured the rest of the team would be on him quickly to pick it up. It took ALL that each of us had for us to win. Whatever it took for us to cross that finish line close together, that's what we did. In other words, part of our code was to do whatever it took to support everyone to win.

We won most of our cross-country meets, or placed very high, even though we had very few superstar runners. We were a championship team. It was my first experience with teams, at the most basic, physical, gut-wrenching level, but the lessons it taught me remain the same today. I have always surrounded myself with people who would push me that way and who would allow me to push as well. It serves them and it serves me. As a result, I have always been blessed with incredibly great friendships, success and wealth. I have also observed that it is in times of pressure, when the stakes are high, that people are transformed. I've NEVER seen a great team that didn't come together without some type of pressure. It could be from competition, from outside influences, or it could be self-induced. We knew in those cross-country meets that every person, every second, every step counted toward a win for our team, and it bound us together. We knew that the success of the team took precedence over our individual goals. No one wanted to let the others down. It drove you as hard as the desire to win. We had a code that said we stuck together no matter what. And in those really important moments, we came together and did what we needed to do to be successful.

Team Tip:

A Code of Honor brings out the best in every person who subscribes to it.

But when pressure increases, sometimes so do emotions. When that happens, intelligence has a tendency to drop. People revert to their base instincts in times of stress, and that's when their true colors come out. Sometimes that's not such a pretty sight. Have you ever said something to someone when you were upset that you wished you had not said a few minutes later? I thought so. That's what I mean about high emotion and low intelligence.

I've seen teams that work well together day to day, but when things get tough, they revert to "every man for himself." A crisis came along and everyone ran for cover, because there was no set of rules to help them see their way through it. Judgments based upon heightened emotions became their guide, which may not turn out to be the best choice for all concerned.

For example, more than half of all marriages end in divorce. In times of stress, the people involved are unable to negotiate their differences. No common code of honor or set of rules holds them together. It is the same issue in the case of a business partnership dispute that has no rules or guidelines. Both situations can get nasty.

It isn't that people don't *want* to work out their differences. The problem is that without rules and expectations mutually agreed upon up front, they act on instinct, particularly when emotions are running high. Each does what he or she thinks is best based upon his or her feelings at the time. Decisions made in that kind of setting may not be the best ones.

Now I know *you've* never been under any kind of stress, right?

Of course you have. You know that when you're upset, when you're under a deadline, when you're angry at a family member or a coworker, it is *impossible* to try to negotiate terms. Why? Because you aren't in your right mind! THAT'S why you need a Code of Honor.

You must create, in a *sane* moment, a set of rules for your team that tell everyone how to operate when the heat is really on. That way, in those moments of high stress, the rules legislate the behavior, rather than the emotions. The Code is NOT just a set of guidelines to be used only when it's convenient. These are rules that must be "called" when breached.

The needs, tasks and problems of a team determine how rigid its code is. The Marine Corps has a code that holds its teams together under fire.

When bullets are flying, life and death may have to take second place to logic and team play. Repetition of their code and its rules conditions the team to come together as a cohesive, trusting unit rather than just running for individual survival.

Having a Code of Honor doesn't mean that everyone on the team is happy 100 percent of the time. Sometimes things get messy. A code can cause upset, create confrontation and even put people on the spot. But ultimately, it protects every member of the team from abuse, neglect and breaches of ethics. A Code of Honor brings out the best in every person who subscribes to it.

You can NEVER assume that people know the code on their own. It isn't something that's necessarily intuitive. You learn it from others—parents, coaches, leaders or friends. Someone has to "show" it to you. And everyone involved must agree to it. This is true for any relationship, be it with your business, your family or yourself—any relationship with an interest in its own happiness and success.

Currently about 50 percent of the gross domestic product of the United States comes from small businesses, and of that, about half of those businesses are sole proprietorships or home-based businesses. I tell you this to emphasize a point: The average person has much more power than you think. The way you conduct your business affects the lives of many others.

Team Tip:

Your code is a reflection of you and will attract those who aspire to the same standards.

Your reputation, your income and your longevity depend upon your consistency of behavior internally and externally. The future of the country is in the hands of those who drive the economy, the markets, our businesses and our families. That's you! Your significance may seem minuscule, but never doubt your influence on others. Your code is a reflection of you and will attract those who aspire to the same standards. How you conduct your business may have a bigger impact than the service you provide.

Decide here and now that you will create a Code of Honor for yourself and for the teams you're a part of. What do you stand for? What code do you publicize to the world? How tight is your team? How happy do you want to be?

My purpose here is to give you steps, motivation and insights to building a great team that will give you and those you touch the wealth, satisfaction and joy that you all deserve. So let's talk about who's on your team.

Team Drill:

1. Discuss great teams that you have been on. What was it like? What were the rules? How did it feel?

2. What would be the benefits to having a code for your business? Your finances? Your health? Your family?

Chapter Two

Who You Surround Yourself With Will Determine Your Wealth and Success— Who's on the Team?

In order to build a cohesive unit, it helps to start with great players. This is true whether you are talking about a business, a nonprofit agency, a club, a down-line, a community, government or even a family. Great players are determined by their talent, desire and willingness to play by the code.

It's true that in some cases you don't have much choice who is in your group. The code, however, allows those who have not yet joined to decide if this is the type of team they want to be on. And for those who are already on the team, it allows them to decide if they want to stay or not.

I know that this seems a bit brutal, but you have to make a decision about whether you are playing to be comfortable or to be liked or if you really want to win. Look, I may want to play football for the Philadelphia Eagles, but that doesn't mean I get to! Do I have what it takes to play on that team? NO!

A great team is not just a group of people with a common objective. It is a group committed to working together toward a common goal in which each person's unique abilities will be tested and stretched to the fullest. They are willing to subordinate themselves to the good of the team and to follow rules that may subject them to scrutiny, correction and review. Teams are not always fun. They can be messy, upsetting and downright pains in the you-know-what. But the results that a great team can accomplish are truly exhilarating. The power, trust and confidence of a hot team are unstoppable.

True teams have a very clear set of priorities:

- Mission first
- Needs of the team second
- Needs of the individual third

In many organizations that I have worked with over the last fifteen years, the priorities were totally reversed. I find that many want to know "What's in it for me?" first. If they're sure that they are getting that, they *might* help someone else on their team, as long as it doesn't infringe on their time, money or effort. And *then* they'll support the mission.

Unfortunately, the reason so many teams wallow in mediocrity is that, regardless of what people say (because anyone can talk a good story!), the mission seems to come last. Personal interests take precedence and the leader, business owner or entrepreneur is faced with fighting the battle alone and hoping to get some support along the way. In reality, most people don't believe that if they take care of the mission first, the rest gets taken care of.

That's no team.

On the Rich Dad team, *elevating the financial well-being of humanity* comes first or you can't be on the team. It's 24/7, and time, money and personal considerations are put aside for the good of the mission and the team. Guess what? In this scenario, everyone wins big. In the other, there are lots of excuses but few results.

I'll give you an example: I used to own an air freight trucking company in California where I had crewmembers working around the clock. We had a deadline for loading trucks—if they weren't loaded and ready to depart by 3:00 a.m., they would not make delivery on time to the East Coast. We had several instances where we had so much freight that our night crew, who loaded those trucks, was falling behind.

By 11:00 p.m., it became apparent that we were not going to make the cutoffs. So in true team fashion, the night crew foreman got on the phone and called up the day crew and asked them to come in to help, even though they had already worked a full shift that day.

Not one person complained about it. The daytime folks took care of the paperwork and the administrative work, so that the night crew could focus its attention on loading those trucks and getting them out on time. Trucks pulled out by 2:45 a.m. and the mission was accomplished. Everyone high-fived, some went to breakfast and the rest went home to bed. We didn't have to do it often, but everyone felt exhilarated and pumped when we did. No one asked for overtime, extra time off or special favors. Mission came first, teammates second and self third. It happened because we had a rule in our Code of Honor that said to "never abandon a teammate in need." Because of that rule, no one felt unsupported, and no one was left behind.

Our company's mission in that situation was to load those trucks and get them out on time. But what is so important to recognize here is that in the attempt to accomplish the mission, the needs of the team, or in this case the night crew, were met. And ultimately, the needs of the individuals were met as well. No one had to feel stressed out or unsupported, because the work got done. We had ourselves a championship team.

But what's also <u>important to recognize is that *the fact that you want to play on a team doesn't mean that you qualify.*</u> So how do you determine who should be on the team?

The Draft: Getting Players on the Team

If desire isn't enough, what should you look for when creating a team? Who are the people you surround yourself with, and will they push you up, hold you to the same standards or bring you down? You have to make that call. As we get older, this gets harder to do, because it may mean breaking habits and a social circle that you've grown comfortable with. There comes to be a feeling of emotional obligation. So the quicker you take a look at who's on your team, the better.

Here are the questions you need to ask yourself when pulling a team together:

1. What kind of energy do they have?

At SalesDogs, the motto is "Highest energy wins!" This is especially true in sales, but also on any team that interfaces with other people. What kind of energy? Engaging, interactive, inquisitive, active, bright and full of possibility. A great team player never thinks or speaks in terms of "can't," only in terms of "how can we?" You know the kind of person I am talking about. In their own way, they light up a room with either excitement and enthusiasm, calmness and focus or strength and confidence. I cannot stress the importance of energy enough, because it permeates everything that you do. It is the source of resourcefulness and connectedness with others and laces the environment with upbeat feelings that increase speed and possibility. Who do you have around you? Think about it. Criticism is okay, in fact imperative, but does it expand the possibilities or contract them?

2. Do they have a desire to win?

One of Rich Dad's rules is that you must have an undying desire to win. Not that you will win all the time, but that you are going for it. Some people just want to be liked, to be comfortable and to be part of a team, and that's great. But do they *want to win?* Are they willing to do what it takes? Lots of people say they want to win, but do they really? It's an easy thing to say, but where are they when the "heat" is on?

Ask yourself, "Do I want to win?" Because why in the world would you have people on your team who are only there to collect a paycheck and hang out, not really caring if the team wins? Sure, everybody *likes* to win. But are they willing to put in the time and energy? I'm not an advocate of hard work for its own sake, but I do advocate doing whatever it takes to get the win. Are they willing to put off immediate gratification for that long-term success?

3. Are they willing to let somebody else win?

Being on a team means that you put aside your desire for immediate personal gain and that you are willing to support others. That means you don't always get to be the star. You have to be okay with sitting on the bench if that's what's best for the team. If someone has a better idea, be willing to listen with an open mind and keep quiet until they complete their thoughts. People who want to know about their salary before they find out the mission are highly suspect.

4. Are they personally responsible?

Another necessary quality for anyone who wants to join a team is the willingness to take responsibility, not blaming others but owning up to mistakes. In your interview, ask any candidate about the biggest mistakes and the biggest wins he or she ever made and why they happened. What went wrong? Did someone else get the blame? Were there circumstances beyond their control? What did this person learn from that experience? Listen very carefully to their answers. You don't want someone on your team who can't take responsibility or who points fingers at others. That breeds distrust, and will destroy your team. You want someone who will say, "I learned something from that," or, "Next time I would do this."

5. Are they willing to submit to the code?

Anyone looking to join your team must understand the current Code of Honor. Once it's explained, he or she can do one of three things:

- Agree with it (great!)
- Disagree with it (in which case this person is a wrong fit for the team)
- Ask questions to clarify

Using my example of the trucking company's code, new candidates would sometimes ask whether they would receive more money for helping the night crew. Our staff would smile and say no and would gently but firmly tell them that our outfit was probably not a good fit for them. It doesn't mean they were bad people, but they just wouldn't fit in a culture that defines "never abandon a teammate in need" the way *we* did.

6. Do they have unique talent or ability?

Ideally each person on the team should be there because of the **unique abilities and talents** that they bring to their positions. Accountants do not need to be artists or copywriters. Salespeople do not need to be technicians. When putting your team together or rearranging an existing one, make sure that you get the best people doing what they do best. Shaquille O'Neal for the LA Lakers is six-foot-ten and 350 pounds. He is a great power forward. He would make a terrible jockey! Get my point? We'll talk more about this later.

Team Tip:

Make sure that anyone coming onto the team has some unique talent that he or she brings to the position. Don't hire to fill space.

Team Checklist:

Qualities of a great team player:

1. Energy
2. Unstoppable desire to win
3. Willing to let someone else win
4. Personally responsible—no blaming or justifying
5. Willing to submit to the code
6. Unique talent or ability

In the end, who is on the team is determined by the standards that you set and the code that you are willing to live by. Once you draw a line in the sand and make clear who you are, what your standards are and what is acceptable and what is not, you will have a lineup of people who want to play that way. You may also have some fallout from those who don't want to play that way in the beginning. And that's okay.

In choosing who is on the team, I tend to follow the advice I heard once from Bill Cosby on one of his shows. He said, *"I don't know the key to success, but I do know that the key to failure is trying to please everyone."*

If you try to accommodate everyone, you will attract a bit of everything. As a result, you will have to deal with all kinds of different neuroses. You have enough on your hands to deal with, and unless you have a degree in psychology, why bother?

Great Expectations

If a person has the energy, willingness to take third priority, the undying desire to do what it takes to win, a willingness to take responsibility, a willingness to adhere to and support the code, and a bit of talent, you have a good start. Make sure that the rules are clear and consistent.

While change is a constant, changing the rules should not be. The code lives on in spite of what happens. The bigger the team gets, the tighter the code needs to be to ensure peak performance. If you are a five-person team in a Phoenix, Arizona, office, the code is easily supported. But as you open offices in New York, London, Singapore, Sydney, Los Angeles, Chicago, and so forth, it gets tougher to hold to the same standards.

Try this experiment: Take about a two- to three-foot piece of kite string and tie a small weight to the end of it. Twirl it above your head as a cowboy would a lasso. Swing it faster. What happens? You have to hold on tighter. Lengthen the string. What happens? You have to hold on even tighter and pick up speed in order to keep the weight aloft.

The same is true of teams as they grow in numbers and spread out geographically. The code has to be stronger, better supported and revisited with more frequency as size increases. You also have to pick up speed or the whole project never gets off the ground. This is backward to what happens as companies grow. They typically get more bureaucratic and slow down.

On the other side of the coin, one of my clients, Singapore Airlines, engages in what some would consider an unreasonable demand on their senior management staff. The incredible number of visits from senior staff to remote stations and regions around the globe continues to reestablish the culture, attitude and code from Singapore itself. Their execs sacrifice time from family and spend countless hours in the air in an incredible commitment to the spirit of that forty-plus-year-old airline. They combine speed, frequency and deep cultural attitudes into an organization that has continued to be rated as the number-one airline in the world, which has also continued to make profit quarter after quarter through even the toughest times in the industry.

In the case of existing teams, the code must be a matter of choice. If people have been on the team for a long time without clear rules, they have to be given a choice to play or not with the new code. It's unfair to spring new rules on people without warning or reasons why. But they do have to choose! It's tough, but remember that in the absence of rules, people play by their own rules. The biggest collisions in life occur because people play by different sets of rules.

Team Tip:

Rules must be consistent and clearly communicated up front so that everyone is clear about expectations. Otherwise there may be differing definitions later that will cause upset.

Everyone has their own sets of rules. That's why you have to have a code, so that everyone plays by the same ones!

The funny thing is that, even in the face of those collisions, both parties will always feel that they are completely justified in their position and that they have done nothing wrong. Why? Because they were playing by *their* rules. Disgruntled employees complain that their boss was too demanding and they end up quitting their jobs because of it. Their rules said, "We do whatever it takes to complete the tasks as long we get paid for everything we do from nine to five and after that it's overtime." Their boss's rules were, "We do whatever it takes to complete the tasks whether we get paid or not." Neither one is right or wrong. That's why you create a code to decide what that means in a sane moment.

The mechanics who work for NASCAR are all very talented and experienced. They have to be. But no matter how much experience they start with, when they are hired, their first duty is to stack tires. You know why? Because not only do they need to understand the importance of every single job performed on that team, but they have to understand this new culture that they're now a part of! As a new team member, they assume a position of *serving others first* ... not of being a star.

When choosing new team players, you have to observe if they are willing to enter the team from a position of serving others and lying low, listening and learning. If they are, you know you have a person who is doing his or her best to earn the right to be a great team member. Every organization has its own set of rules, its own way of doing things. A clear understanding of expectations and rules is critical for anyone joining *any* kind of team. Without it, I wouldn't want to be in the car that the new mechanic worked on, and neither would you!

Playing Strengths

We've talked about building a team by asking important questions, determining motivation and setting expectations. But the next component is perhaps the most important in knowing who's on the team. If you remember nothing else from this book, remember this: The key to success is playing to people's strengths.

When was the last time you were given a "performance evaluation" at work? I'll bet I can tell you what happened. You were shown a sheet of paper that listed your strengths and your weaknesses. And what were you told to do? Improve your weaknesses.

I am here to tell you, that is a *colossal* waste of time. It's hard enough to figure out what you are really good at. Why waste your time trying to fix something that you may be chromosomally programmed *not* to do? Why on earth would you tell someone to do something he's lousy at?

A great team is a group of people who all play to their own unique strengths with a Code of Honor holding them tightly together. One of Rich Dad's core concepts is that when you take on a business partner, you look for someone with a *unique ability*. Why? Because you complement each other, you fill in each other's gaps and ultimately increase the value, quality and versatility of your product or service.

Want to create a championship team from scratch? Find out what each member is great at. Not just good or competent at, but *great*. And when you're done, you've got yourself a team that is *great* at what they do, but also satisfied and confident. Everyone wins.

Again, the same is true for families. For instance, in the partnership my wife and I share, I work with the business, sales and generating income. That's my unique ability. But my wife's unique ability in the business is her eye for detail. She can also spot patterns in an instant. She is also a *great* mom, and she is passionate about educating our kids. We are a successful partnership, and we each bring something different and unique to the table.

You may not be able to control whether everyone on your team gets to play to their strengths, but you can control who you're around.

Are you around people who are disgruntled with what they do? Are you in a job where nobody likes what they do, but they stay because they need the paycheck? That's a scenario to bring your energy down, and you will never win. Put yourself in situations where people are "jamming" because they're doing what they do best. People who love numbers are crunching numbers, creative people are being creative, people who love to sell are selling, and so forth. If you surround yourself with people like that, the energy will continue to go up.

Conditioning

One of the problems with building great teams is that people aren't taught to work on teams. In school, we were taught to do things on our own. Cooperation in the classroom was viewed as cheating.

When you were in school, do you remember being graded on the curve? Whoever got the highest grade, no matter what that actual score was, got an A. Not such a bad thing if everyone got a bad grade, right? But that one person who actually did well on the test did so at the expense of his or her classmates.

We were told not to ask our friends for help with our homework. That was considered cheating. Who read our research papers? No one but the teacher, of course. So we got no input from anyone else about how good our papers were, or whether they were even interesting. No one had a vested interest in helping anyone else improve or do better. As a matter of fact, if you were graded on the curve, you hoped others would do badly. Not a great way to promote collaboration and cooperation.

Then we got out into the world and got jobs. Your experience was probably the same as mine. Your boss told you what to do, and you did it; not much questioning, no working with a coworker to accomplish the task at hand. If you couldn't get the job done, you were fired. No one was going to do the job for you, and if you needed help, maybe you weren't competent to have the job in the first place.

Sound familiar?

Remember the old concept, "If you want it done right, you have to do it yourself!"? Imagine a group of folks trying to complete a project as a team all coming from that point of view!

Many people aren't conditioned to work on teams. It's a hard mindset to change. It's wasted energy to be worrying if your teammates might bring you down, or worrying about confronting them if something goes wrong.

Dr. Jerry B. Harvey, author of *The Abilene Paradox* and professor in Management Science at The George Washington University, defines cheating as *"the failure to assist others if they request it."* Why? Because by only taking care of yourself, you actually jeopardize the results of the whole. There is no way that you can out produce a great team on your own. If you fail to support, everyone loses. That's cheating!

Working on a team that has a tight Code of Honor gets people out of that prior "non-team" conditioning, and helps them become better players.

Getting Along with Each Other

To work effectively together, any team needs to be able to communicate well with each other. I've learned that there are four components for building understanding and rapport within a team:

1. Everyone in the group must have a genuine interest in the mission of the team and in the well-being of the other team members.

Those aren't just words. If you are on a team, or even in your family, your best chance of gaining cooperation and understanding from others is to show genuine respect and care for them. You've heard the expression, "Do unto others as you would have them do unto you." I don't always agree with that expression, because there are some people who treat themselves badly! You don't have to love them ... just show some genuine care for them. The easiest way to do this is simply to take the time to acknowledge others for their efforts and accomplishments even if they are small. Simply a "thank you," "well done," "you're awesome," once in a while will do. (If the little voice in your head is right now feeling uncomfortable with this, work on it!) If you ever want to create wealth and harmony in your life, the law of reciprocity says that you have to be willing to give first. It is one of the biggest differences between S's and B's.

2. There needs to be a shared reality. You have to be able to talk to people in *their* terms first, and in *their* language.

Do your best to talk to teammates based upon what is going on for them, not you. Speak not in response to what they say, but to what they're thinking. BIIIIIG difference. Have you ever noticed that people say one thing and do something very different? You can avoid that by addressing what you think they are thinking rather than what they are saying. Let them know that you want to understand and are willing to listen and your communication will be much more meaningful. Everyone wants to talk about *their* experience. Have you ever come back from a vacation and someone asked you how it went and within two minutes they are blabbing all about *their* similar experience? Don't do that! Shut up, engage and listen. You will be amazed at the response if you are willing to step into someone else's reality and stay there for a while.

3. It's important to articulate what you want to say clearly and *briefly*.

Just get to the point. Brief enough?

4. Ask for duplication and duplicate for others. Verify that you've been heard by asking the person to repeat what you said and vice versa.

What you meant isn't necessarily what was *heard*. By the way, this works in reverse too. Repeat to others your understanding of what they said and get verification. I know I have misunderstood others way more than once. How about you? Some of the biggest upsets in families, some of the best deals that went awry and some of the most powerful missed opportunities occur not because of bad people, but simply by not understanding.

Team Checklist:

Factors to ensure optimum team communication:

- Display true interest in the team and each other in all communications.

- Talk to others in their terms and in their language.

- Be brief, clear and to the point!

- Verify all communications through repetition or duplication of what was said.

Because a bunch of people are working in the same place doesn't mean they're a team. Several factors must be in place. What result do you want to achieve? What code, or set of behaviors, must be in place to achieve it? What mindset, attitude, talents and unique abilities do the members of the team possess? And what is their prior conditioning? I call this my Results Model:

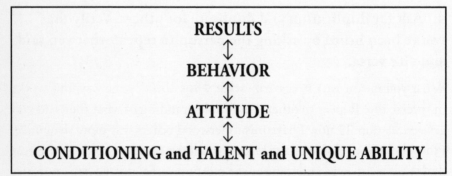

RESULTS
↕
BEHAVIOR
↕
ATTITUDE
↕
CONDITIONING and TALENT and UNIQUE ABILITY

These four components are inextricably linked, as both causes and effects, because they are constantly reinforcing each other. What results do you want? Your behavior, attitude and conditioning will contribute to achieving them. This model is the core of all businesses, and it is the core of building success in your family and your business (and yourself!).

I once asked one of my clients, from Deutsche Bank, what was the biggest lesson he got from one of our programs. He said it was this model. He said, "I learned that if you focus on results you're too late! No one ever got obese eating one piece of chocolate cake!" He went on to say that as a result of this model, his approach to his team had become very different. Rather than pounding only on results, he looked at the attitudes, activities and behavior of his direct reports. He found that he could head off problems earlier and ensure success more easily by coaching his team at levels further down the model (behavior, attitude, conditioning).

Team Tip:

Results are always a function of behavior, attitude and conditioning. If you focus on results, you are too late!

Now ask yourself: Would *you* be on your team? Would *you* choose you? Would you choose all the people that are close to you? If you could wipe the slate clean and start over again, would you choose the same people? If the answer's no, I suggest you start by creating a code and giving them a choice to step up or look around for a new team, because it's only a matter of time before your current team falls apart anyway.

If the answer's yes, you may have the makings of a championship team. You can go a long way on your own, but you eventually need a team to support you, to give you that kick in the behind sometimes, to push you, to call you and themselves on the rules, who have good energy and are in it to win. And your Code of Honor will continue to pull you even more tightly together.

So now let's talk about how to create your Code of Honor.

Team Drill:

1. Discuss old beliefs that do not support team behavior and how they could affect you—particularly under pressure.

2. Make a list of the traits you want for anyone coming onto your team. If you were to assemble a dream team for your business, who would they be if money was no object? Now go get them or get those with the same talents, attitudes and abilities.

3. Make a large chart of the results model on a large sheet of paper and hang it somewhere where your team can see it all the time. Refer to it often to reinforce the results that you want.

4. Take a few moments as a team or with individual members of your team to tell each other what you think the other person's unique talent or ability is. Don't talk about what they are not good at. Listen without response and notice what the "little voice" in your head says. Acknowledge what you hear and do not offer rebuttal. Do the same thing at home.

5. Make a point to be responsible for your communication. Hang a poster that says: "True Communication Is the Response That You Get!"

Chapter Three

Creating a Code of Honor That Brings Out the Best

Obviously, if you are going to create the code with your existing team, you need to know who's really on the team before you sit down and try to create your Code of Honor. It's these standards that, if created and agreed upon by the *entire* team, will hold that team together, especially when the pressure is on and challenges arise.

If you are starting from scratch, without a team, get clear on your code first. At that point you can begin attracting those who are predisposed to agree with you.

Unfortunately, however, most people don't really know who's on their team until they *are* under pressure, and by that time it's too late to start negotiating. That's why creating these standards, or rules, ahead of time is important. It creates a framework so that everyone understands how to treat each other not only in good times, but in times of challenge as well.

These rules define things like professionalism, team play, integrity and communication, among other things. You will have to decide at what level of performance you want to operate—the tighter your code, the higher your level of performance.

Whether you are talking physics, sports, relationships or wealth, there is a generalized principle that the tighter the tolerance, the higher the performance. Let me give you an analogy.

My first car in high school was a 1963 Chevy Nova convertible. The maximum speed of that car was about fifty miles an hour, downhill. I loved that car, but let's face it, this was not a high-performance vehicle.

Now on the other hand, my wife used to work for Northrop, a company that made F-18 fighter planes, like the ones you saw in *Top Gun*. Obviously a much better piece of machinery than my little Chevy. Rivets are actually packed in dry ice before being inserted into the fuselage of the aircraft. The manufacturing tolerances are very tight due to the incredible speeds, altitudes and maneuvers required of the plane.

Imagine what would happen if you tried to move my old car through space at Mach 3! It would disintegrate! By the same token, driving an F-18 at fifty miles an hour down a runway will never get it off the ground.

The problem is there are many organizations, teams and groups that want to perform like an F-18 but are operating at the tolerance level of a Chevy Nova! Simply wanting to be a championship team or desiring to operate at peak levels isn't enough. If you take your team, your family or your group to the limits without tight rules, they will blow apart when the going gets tough.

Team Tip:

The higher the performance, the tighter the tolerances need to be.

The reason that the Marines have a rigid Code of Honor is that when bullets are whizzing by your head, emotion tends to be high and intelligence low. The code is drilled into the group over and over to hold them together under pressure; it does not allow them to run for cover to save their own skins. In that example, it's a matter of life or death. There have to be rules in place that ensure that each individual does the right things in order to protect the team and each other.

The same is true with your company, or your family. The growth or death of your business may depend upon how you handle difficult times. This is certainly true with your kids and your family. There may be times when team members want to cover their own behinds instead of doing what's best for the whole. That's natural. It's based upon our conditioned responses. Yet to move to the next level of commitment and connectedness with your family, your spouse or your team, that same behavior can kill the best efforts. The code holds them accountable to each other and the mission.

Every family and every marriage goes through trying times. The code or the rules keep them united. Otherwise kids go off and make their own decisions, which may not be in their best interest. Spouses can get distracted or stressed, and under pressure they may say and do things that they regret later. The code is the set of agreements and rules that force you to be the person that you agreed you wanted to be in a sane and logical moment.

You have to decide at what level you want to play. Lemonade stand on the corner or a hot, winning enterprise? Convenient relationship or life-long devoted marriage? A bunch of folks dabbling in a mutual interest or a championship team?

Your code will determine your level of play, but it will also be what brings new people to your team. The stronger the code, the greater its attractive power. It acts like a beacon that attracts others of the same mindset. The clearer you are about it, the more people of like mind will be attracted to it.

If you don't enjoy taking orders, shaving your head or shooting automatic weapons . . . don't join the Marines! But people there love it! It's not that one code serves all, or that one is better than the other. Each person has his own set of values and is attracted to a different code. The culture and code of Singapore Airlines is different from that of United Airlines. The Catholic Church is different from the Presbyterian Church. It's a matter of preference, but once you sign up, you are expected to support those rules.

All great relationships have rules that all parties agree to. This is true in business, sports, personal relationships and families.

I will be the first say that I am *no* marriage counselor. Nor do I want to be one. But it is not a surprise that nearly 50 percent of all marriages don't last. It's partly because many couples have no clear agreements or each partner operates by his or her own personal rules. At the first sign of stress, people revert to their own rules.

My wife, Eileen, and I have a code. Why? Because it is the most important team in our lives! We want to preserve it and thrive in it. These are of some of our rules:

- Communicate daily no matter where I am in the world. (I travel a lot!)

- Stick with all disagreements until they are resolved.

- Study together.

- Keep your agreements.

- Commit to personal development and education.

Those rules are good for any team . . . at home or at work.

So think about the teams in your life: at home, at work or in your community. What message do you want to send and what impact do you want to have on others?

Steps for Creating a Code of Honor

There are several steps in creating a Code of Honor:

1. Find a *sane* moment in which to create the code.

I've said this before, but it can't be stressed enough. Do not wait until the pressure is high, emotions are running hot, there's a deadline to meet or the heat is really on. It must be in a moment when everyone is thinking clearly and rationally. Most people try to create, legislate and execute rules in the heat of the battle. Bad idea! Remember, high emotion and low intelligence. All you will do in that case is create an uglier fight. If you find yourself in that situation, call a time-out and table the rule making for a sane time.

Also, don't expect to do this all in one sitting. That you found a sane moment doesn't mean you should expect to take care of everything during that time. There needs to be a lot of thought put into the creation of the code, and it's also important not to burn everyone out. It could take days, weeks or even months.

It might be a good idea to find a time when you can actually leave the office. Get away from ringing phones and an inbox that's piling up. People tend to think more clearly when they're away from work. I'm not saying you have to take a retreat to Hawaii to do this (although I'm sure no one would complain!), but maybe you get a conference room at a nearby hotel and order in sandwiches. Whatever it takes so that people are relaxed and thinking clearly for this process. The point is to be thinking in your highest state.

A client of mine sells and distributes hair care products all over the world. We have been working on the code for their performing artists for nearly two months. It will probably be another several months until we finish the first draft. Going back and forth and defining each of the rules will require discussion and debate. That's a good thing! I will give you an example in a minute.

2. Find recurring issues that repeatedly interfere with the performance of the team.

I was once asked by a global investment bank to work with a bunch of floor traders. This was a very intelligent, adept, fast-moving, arrogant and cocky bunch of people. They operated like a band of roving gunslingers, and it was my job to help them become a championship team!

One of the rules they came up with in their Code of Honor said, "Public humiliation is not allowed on the trading floor." This was a very important rule for them. Why? Because in the chaotic high-pressure environment of the trading floor, tempers and emotions can run high. When back office folks came onto the floor to help execute trades made by the traders, some of the traders would yell, scream and take the heads off the back office folks for even the littlest of reasons. This was hugely disruptive to productivity, not to mention feelings. Plus it disrupted other team members who were trying to conduct business. It also set up "getting even" scenarios later on! They had identified this as a recurring problem and decided it was important enough to write a rule about it.

With the rule in place, the team policed itself to uphold the standard. Guess what? Productivity and seamless operation between front and back office improved immediately and dramatically. During a time on Wall Street when markets were taking a huge hit, this team out produced every other trading team around the world in the bank simply because they had learned how to come together as a team instead of looking only for their own interests.

Your code needs to address your particular needs, your particular team's mission and your particular recurring problems. And it shouldn't just deal with special cases, like "last week Frank did this to Mary, so let's make a rule about it." Find recurring, regularly appearing issues that your team faces. Is perpetual lateness an issue for your team? Do people have a hard time keeping agreements? Is there a lot of finger-pointing, gossiping and so forth? You can create rules that deal with these things. Try to look beyond the symptoms to the real, underlying problems.

Also, take a look not only at what's *not* working, but also at what *is* working. For instance, does your team really come together well under pressure, step up to the plate and get the job done? Do they spontaneously celebrate each other's wins? Isolate good behaviors such as these, and then find out what prevents this behavior from happening on a consistent basis.

Here is a sample code:

1. Never abandon a teammate in need.
2. Be willing to "call" and "be called." (We'll talk about what this is and how to do it in the next chapter.)
3. Celebrate all wins!
4. Be on time.
5. Keep all agreements and clean up any broken or potentially broken agreements ASAP.
6. Deal direct. (If you have a problem with someone go directly to that person with it or get off it!)
7. Be responsible—no laying blame on others, no justifications!

8. Be resourceful—find solutions before "dumping" on others.
9. Never let personal "stuff" get in the way of your mission.
10. Be loyal to the team.
11. Commit to personal development.
12. Don't seek or ask for sympathy or acknowledgment.
13. Everyone must sell!

You can tell from our code that we are a personal development and sales organization. Most of our rules deal with being the best that we can be inside and out!

What's vital to your team? You and your team have to figure that out.

3. *Everyone* participates!

If you are creating a code for an existing team, it is critical to get everyone involved for two reasons. First, if they create it, they own it. Second, it allows those who do not like the new rules to opt out in the process. This can save you lots of grief later. Face it, some people cannot stand to be accountable to others, or to themselves for that matter. If you get everyone involved in the process, players get a chance to opt in or out along the way. They can never say that they had no say in the matter and whine about it later.

One financial services firm that I worked with had a line in its code that read, "Never abandon a teammate in need." To them, that meant that you had to be willing to offer support to each other unconditionally. It meant that if you're finished with your work and your teammate is still stuck facing a deadline, you stay and offer support. That doesn't necessarily mean that you do their work for them. But it does mean that if they need a cup of coffee, a photocopy or moral support, you offer them whatever they need to get the job done. And it doesn't matter who you are: Whether you're the boss or the janitor, the code applies.

This rule created a lot of controversy with this team. In the discussion, one person popped up and said, "Why should I be penalized for someone else's incompetence or laziness?" And honestly, that's a fair question, and that person had the right to ask it. That's great discussion!

The hard questions have to be asked in order to clarify the rule. It leaves nothing to chance. If and when everyone agrees to it, it is because everyone is crystal clear on what it means.

A word about disagreements. They are great. They are the stuff that forges great teams. Yet after the smoke clears, if everyone doesn't agree, be careful. If, after all the discussions, someone still feels it's a compromise, you as a team will have to make a decision. You can either:

- Change the rule,
- Throw it out, or
- Ask the opposing team member(s) to go elsewhere.

If you leave that rule unresolved, I guarantee that it will come back to haunt you. And it will be ugly and uncomfortable, and you will be forced to deal with it later anyway, possibly when the stakes are higher!

As a facilitator, watch for anyone in the group who seems to be holding back, or isn't giving full attention to the process. You must call it *immediately*. You have to get any withholding of opinions, feelings and thoughts out in the open or it will undermine the group later. Remember, you're creating a code that gets people to participate on a team. It can't just be to appease a few people. If you think someone's faking it, call them on that, too! Point out that this code is intended to protect everyone on the team. This isn't an enforcement mechanism, and it's not a way to keep people contained. It's a protection measure that allows everyone to do their best work.

Nearly every time I work with intact teams, I get "briefed" on the team and invariably get told about the "problem children" on the team. You know what I mean. It's that one person who always seems to buck the trend, upset the status quo, not get with the program ... I usually smile and let the client know that I will suspend my judgment until I see them operate and until we start forming the code.

In most cases, even though this person opposes a commonly agreed-upon rule, and seems to be digging in his heels just to be contradictory, there is more to the story. What I've found is that many of these cases stem not from this person trying to be difficult, but from his history with this issue, something that this person is having a hard time communicating.

Dig deeper. Maybe this person isn't very good at expressing his particular set of standards or values. Maybe he's hanging on to some troublesome past incident. If someone is being resistant, don't back off, keep digging and working with this person until a comfort level is reached or until it becomes clear that he or she wants to opt out.

I have found many times that the problem child was really a person with extremely high standards but without the ability to communicate well with others. In an effort to improve performance, this person grated on people's nerves and alienated himself.

Many of us really have similar values and beliefs. We all want to work hard, provide for our families, be happy and have good relationships. A great thing about this whole process is that you get to find out how much you really have in common with your teammates, and that will only help you all in the long run.

I understand that sometimes it's hard to get everyone together to talk at the same time. With one of my clients we faced the challenge of instituting the creation of a code with about thirty-five thousand employees. Well, obviously there's no way we were going to get thirty-five thousand people together. But in a situation like this, what you can do is have the key people from each department get together, to voice the concerns of their respective departments. Then it filters through those key people to the employees in those departments, and then those folks eventually get to offer their feedback.

Issuing a code from the top down and expecting everyone to buy into it is unrealistic. People need to feel ownership, which requires everyone's involvement. As we went region by region, the same issues and the same code items repeated themselves. That's normal. We allowed each region or department to have its own codes. As a result, struggling offices came into alignment and in one case one of the busiest offices with the worst numbers became the third-highest producer in the company. With the creation of the code, some people left, new ones came in and they got serious!

4. Talk about various instances of behavior, and how everyone felt about them, both positively and negatively.

I find myself constantly surprised in my time working with teams that people can work together for ten or fifteen years and still not know how their teammates feel about certain issues. Use this opportunity to talk about times these issues were abused or acknowledged.

This goes back to getting everyone's involvement. Sometimes through talking about a rule, you'll uncover deep-seated resentments and resolve a lot of problems. Sometimes the simplest issues leave the deepest scars.

Working with a community hospital, we assisted the various departments in creating their individual and hospital-wide codes of honor. In working with the surgery team, it took us nearly an hour to decide what "Be on time" meant! For years it meant different things to different people. To some it meant to clock in on time. To others it meant being clocked in, scrubbed, dressed and ready to work on time. The difference between the two definitions was at least ten minutes. And in those ten minutes the "little voice" in everyone's head would go into daily finger-pointing. "Why is that person always late?" While on the other side people were saying to themselves, "Why are they looking at me funny? I know they are trying to make me feel guilty," and so forth.

The problem with this unsaid stuff is that it gets acted out later in the form of rude comments, bad attitudes or omitted details. Whenever there is resentment, sooner or later there is revenge. Since they aired the issue and haggled through the discussion, they came up with a common definition and back-biting disappeared just from a simple discussion.

This is why you must talk about the pros and cons of every issue and get to the root of people's feelings before agreeing on any rule.

5. As soon as you are able to decide on a rule, *write it down!*

Post the rules in a viewable place, where everyone on the team can see them every day, like a break room or an office. My family's code at home is posted on our refrigerator. Under pressure it might be easy to forget the rules: out of sight, out of mind. Put them right out front, where everyone, including your customers, can see them. Sure, it might be kind of hokey, but it works.

The rules should be stated clearly enough so that anyone could explain them. Remember, once a code is in place, everyone owns it, and it had better be understood clearly.

6. Be specific!

Your rules must be written as statements, rules or agreements that can be acted on. Avoid any vague rules. This may take some doing. You will probably go back and forth about how to phrase your rules. But it's important to get them right.

Let me be very clear on this: A Code of Honor is *not* a mission statement. It is not a list of values. Simply putting a list on the wall that says, "1. Teamwork, 2. Integrity," and so forth is not the same as creating a Code of Honor. Why? Because everyone has a different idea about what teamwork or integrity are. If you spell it out as a statement that someone can act on, you don't run the risk of different interpretations. Instead of "teamwork," maybe you make a rule that says, "The goals of the team come before the individual." That is more clearly defined.

The same goes for rules like "Be professional," "Respect each other" or "Be responsible." How do *you* define "professional"? It depends on your team, on the mission, on the clientele you work with and all kinds of other things. Talk about each person's ideas of concepts like these. Remember my story about the surgical team? The definition of "late" for one person may be very different from someone else's. Clarify, clarify, clarify.

7. Don't try to legislate moods.

Creating a rule that says "Always be in a good mood" or "Never get angry" is not only unfair, it's unrealistic. *Everyone* has bad days. Don't you?

But what you *can* do is say, "Don't take out your bad mood on other people." It's okay to have a lousy day and be in a crappy mood, but it's *not* okay if you dump it on others. That's a reasonable rule that you can act on.

8.   Make sure that the rules are somewhat of a "stretch."

By this I mean that your code challenges everyone on the team to be better. This will create an environment in which everyone gives their best, and the team performs at the championship level.

As I've pointed out, being on a team doesn't mean that every day is a walk in the park. Teams are messy. Rules are messy. Following the rules sometimes means that sacrifices are being made, and that's hard to do. But because this is a challenge, the team becomes better, and the individuals on the team become better, too.

9.   Don't get carried away making rules!

Sure, it's great to deal with problems by making rules about them. But the more rules your team needs, the more screwed up your team is!

Try to shoot for a dozen rules or fewer. Any more than that and your team may feel that they are being micromanaged, and that their behavior is being legislated way too much.

If it seems like you're making too many rules, look for common threads. Is it possible to condense them all into one simple rule? If you really look, you will see a common issue lurking below the surface. Recently a client could not get to less than eighteen rules. Wow! As I sat with the management team and reviewed them there was a common but unstated issue. It seemed that all the rules that the teams had collaborated on alluded to the fact that they felt afraid to speak the truth in front of one another for fear of retribution later. Aha!

We then scrapped the list and started over. A rule about being "willing to listen to another person's opinions and point of view all the way through without interruption" and an agreement to "never engage in comebacks" cut the list dramatically. You have to get to the truth.

A while back, the Rich Dad Advisors team sat down to create a code. We spent a lot of time revising, making rules, revising them again. We went back and forth over, "Don't do this, don't do that, this is okay, but only when..." and so on. All of a sudden someone pointed out that we had *way* too many rules. It turned out that we were able to condense all of these rules into one: "Don't mess with the brand." It answered all of our concerns, and it kept the process and the code from becoming burdensome.

Don't fine-tune your code to add rules; fine-tune for clarity.

Team Checklist:

Steps for creating a Code of Honor:

1. Create the code in a "sane" environment.

2. Isolate recurring behavior that interferes with optimal team performance. This becomes the basis for creating the code. Do the same with behavior that supports team performance.

3. If you have an existing team, get everyone involved.

4. Discuss various instances of productive and nonproductive behavior and how everyone felt about them.

5. From the discussions, *write down* the rules that will support optimal behavior and performance.

6. Make sure that the rules are specific and enforceable without ambiguity, and that they are not general value statements.

7. Don't attempt to legislate moods in the code.

8. Rules should be a challenge and a stretch for everyone.

9. Don't make too many rules. A dozen or fewer is ideal.

10. When someone breaches the code ... "Call it!"

---

10. If someone breaches the code, *call it!*

It's that simple. How? You pull him or her aside and say, "You broke the code."

Lots of families, teams and businesses have rules. But very few "call it" when the code is breached. That is probably the largest distinction between being a good team and being a great team.

It sounds easy, and it can become very easy, but in the beginning, it's not always as easy as it sounds. That's why in most places, it doesn't happen. People don't like to be told they've screwed up. Criticism is awfully hard for most people to take due to lots of emotional garbage that we pick up over the years.

When I say "call it," I don't mean that the person gets chastised. I have not seen punishments, fines, or public humiliation work really well... that's not what I mean. You just acknowledge the breach.

I'll talk more about strategies for doing this in another chapter. But suffice it to say that "calling it" is vital to the strength of a team. The team has to police itself. If a rule is broken and no one calls attention to it, no one takes the code, or the team, seriously. Soon you'll have an even worse environment because not only are there no standards to follow, but there's resentment that no one held up their end of the bargain.

Team Tip:

It's not the job of the boss or team leader to enforce the code, either. The *entire* team enforces it. After all it's "our team"!

What to Expect

So now you've all spent days, weeks or even months creating this Code of Honor. You've determined the problematic issues, you've all communicated with each other effectively, you've condensed several rules into a handful, you've written them down and you've posted them in a prominent place. Life should be perfect now, right?

You're getting there...

I always remind teams I work with that it may get worse before it gets better. And it will get better, eventually, but in the beginning, expect fallout.

It's ironic, but often what you'll see is that after all the talk, after the rules have been hashed out and the code is solidified, it occurs to people, "Oh, I guess it's for real now. I could actually get called on one of these rules." And then they'll jump ship.

Or, on the other side of the coin, you'll have those people who feel the need to test the code immediately.

I'll use my son as an example. He does this to me all the time. He'll pick something up and I'll say, "Put that down!" And he won't. And then I say, "I'm going to count to five, and you have until five to put that down!"

If you have kids, you know exactly what he does. He waits until the very second I say "Five!" to put it down. He has to test me! Well, I'm sorry to say that there is a part of us that never really outgrows that. Something happens to some people the minute you put up rules—they have to test them! Sometimes it's totally unconscious.

At one corporation, I worked with a team to develop a Code of Honor. It took us a few sessions to develop it, but we'd finally completed the process. And within twenty-four hours of completing it, a high-ranking executive breached the code! Part of him had to test it. I swear that it was completely unconscious behavior.

This is a great story because there is a huge point to be made here. Someone—yes, even you—will sooner or later breach the code. Maybe more than once. That is normal. The breaking of the rule is not as important as how it gets handled!

In this case, the team immediately came together. The perpetrator owned it without question and publicly apologized to the group and offered a series of actions to clean it up. The fact that it was addressed instantly and handled by the team publicly sent a powerful message to the rest of the organization. Other teams in the field immediately snapped into accountability. At a recent convention held by that company, the team spirit and energy was incredible! They know they have an awesome team.

This was a great outcome. But understand that people will opt out, act out, get upset for no reason ... expect this. They've agreed to be accountable and it scares them.

This isn't bad, though. It forces people to grow, to be challenged and to become better people who are accountable and responsible. That's a good thing. Once that initial fallout happens, you'll see who's really in it for the long haul, and that's when the magic kicks in.

Dealing with Change

Time changes things. People come and go. Responsibilities sometimes shift with a changing economy. You'll need to expect that, too. Remember, everyone has a code, whether they know it or not. Every person, every team every business has a code. And in the absence of some agreed-upon rules, people will make up their own. When groups merge or new players are added, the rules need to be discussed and reviewed again. As a team adds new people, they don't usually get a voice in the code. It's already there. It is simply for them to understand it and agree to it.

Sample Rules:

- Be willing to stand behind the purpose, rules and goals of the team once decided.

- Speak supportively and with good purpose.

- Acknowledge whatever is being said as true for the speaker at that moment.

- Complete your agreements (responsibility).

- Make only agreements that you are willing and intend to keep.

- Communicate any potential broken agreement at the first appropriate time.

- Clear up any broken agreement at the first opportunity.

- If a problem arises, first look to the system for corrections and then communicate your solution to the person who can do something about it.

- Do not go behind people's backs with problems.
- Be effective and efficient. (Do more with less!)
- Have the willingness to win and allow others to win. (Play win/win.)
- Focus on what works.
- When in doubt check feelings and intuition.
- Agree to work toward an agreement.
- Take personal responsibility. No laying blame, justification or finger-pointing.
- Actively celebrate and acknowledge all wins.
- Always be willing to "do whatever it takes" to win!
- Act first and debrief later. Do not let personal issues stand in the way of your post or task.
- Clarify your own communications and verify the response.
- Be willing to do whatever it takes to support any and all team members.
- Have a willingness to stay together.
- Do not desire or seek sympathy or acknowledgment.
- Keep time agreements!
- Never abandon a teammate in need.
- Support early, often and unconditionally.

We're all human, and rules will get broken. It's inevitable. And later on in the book, we'll talk about how to deal with this.

Team Drill:

Create a Code of Honor for your team!

Chapter Four

What's Your Personal Code?

Greatness doesn't happen by chance, nor does it occur in a vacuum. Greatness comes from, first, a passion for what you do; and second, a clear understanding of what you can and want to be best at. The third component involved in any great story about someone going from rags to riches, overcoming adversity, or achieving success in any area of life is a personal Code of Honor, a set of personal rules and agreements that they are unwilling to compromise.

Do you have a Code of Honor *for you*? What are your rules? To what do you hold yourself accountable? Who the heck are you? You see, because when all the smoke clears, they can take away your money, your possessions, your friends and even your health, and what you are left with is your honor.

In those terms, what is your Code of Honor? I have found that the most powerful people are not always found on the cover of *Newsweek, Fortune Magazine or Sports Illustrated*. Sometimes they may be sitting in the office next door. They are those who have decided in life to take a stand about who they are, what their standards are and who they want to be without regrets.

My suggestion is this: If you haven't done so already, sit down and look at your financial life, your health, your relationships and your values, and create your code. What are you willing to commit to for yourself and your family? What do you stand for?

The problem is that lots of people talk a good story and tell others what they believe in, but in reality don't always live it. It's like the parent who tells his kids not to lie, but cheats on his tax return or fibs to his spouse about where he was or what he was doing. Kids notice. They pick up on it. So they understand that the real code in that case is not "Tell the truth." It's "Don't get caught!" Those messages are sent all day long in the workplace as well.

Great athletes get to where they are because of talent, but also because they set extremely high physical standards for themselves. They commit to hours of practice, working out, being coached, studying their game and taking care of their bodies (well, sometimes!). Most important, set the rules for yourself and don't compromise on yourself.

Team Tip:

What are you willing to hold yourself accountable to?

The reason most people don't have a Code of Honor for themselves is that they don't want to be accountable. They'd rather sleep in than drag themselves out of bed before dawn to go work out, even though they know they should do it. It's called discipline.

Years ago, I was the head student manager for the Ohio State University football team under a very controversial coach by the name of Woody Hayes. He was much maligned by the press and had some fatal quirks that ultimately cost him his career and reputation, but for most of his life he was a great builder of character for thousands of young men.

When he recruited a new player from high school, he would first visit the home of that athlete to get to know the family. What most people don't know about him is that he was looking for two things. Number one, was there discipline in the house? In other words, were there rules—a Code of Honor? Someday, when there was little time left on the game clock and many yards to go for the winning score, would that young fellow have the internal discipline to focus, not panic, and stick to the game plan together with his team?

Woody also was looking for a second component. He wanted to observe whether that young fellow was really loved in his family. Seems strange for a football coach to require that of his players, but very wise. Why? Because it builds self-esteem. It builds an inner confidence that he is not only wanted and valuable to the family or the team, but willing to be supported. Love, as the late coach Vince Lombardi said, is the "heart power" of any team. It is the respect and trust that we give to one another that in the heat of the moment creates championship results.

What's it like at your house?

Why do I mention this? First of all, it's valuable to know for building and supporting your own teams and families. But even more important is that to be the best that *you* can be, you have to care enough about yourself to not let yourself down. If you do not have the discipline, it means at some level that you don't love you! Why in the world would you make an agreement with yourself and not hold yourself accountable to it? It means your health, your wealth and your relationships.

I'm sure you, at one time or another, have had a friend or a colleague come to you with a personal or career-related challenge. And as a good friend you are there to offer advice. You might say things like, "Well I'd never put up with that!" or "This is what you ought to do" or "You should put your foot down!" But what do you do when it comes to you? What are the standards and values that you set for yourself? And are you willing to put *your* foot down and not compromise those standards? Can you honestly say that you *live* it?

You have to have the discipline or the rules in those critical areas of your life and you have to be willing to not only call yourself on breaches of that code, but surround yourself with friends, family or colleagues who will also hold you accountable to your code. If you have the courage to do this, you will not only fulfill your destiny of delivering whatever your true talents are, but you will surround yourself with people who truly love you very, very much, while eliminating those who don't.

So I ask you, what is your code? Is it one of honor or not? Because when all is stripped away, what we are left with and what we leave behind is a record of our actions, our deeds and our impact on others. You have a great code inside you. Be clear on it and don't compromise yourself on it. Don't try to be all things to all people. When you are clear about who you are and what you stand for and you act congruently within that Code of Honor, people of like mind will be attracted to you in droves. You do that and you will build wealth in all areas of your life. My hope is that if you do nothing else after reading this book, you will sit down and set your own Code of Honor.

So what is the code as it relates to your:

- Primary relationship (s)
- Financial freedom
- Business and team
- Family
- Health
- Personal growth

All these things have one thing in common—you. The moment you make the commitment to your Code of Honor, to making those necessary changes, your life will change for the better. And I'm betting that if you're the kind of person to pick up this book, you're someone who is interested in growth and in becoming successful, and you're the kind of person people respect. People look to you and take their cues from what you do, whether you like it or not. Ultimately you *are* your code.

Personal Team Drill:

Sit down in a quiet moment in your favorite place and create your own Code. Think about what's *really* important to you. What problems or patterns have you created for yourself in the past that you'd like to resolve, once and for all, and finally take control of?

For example, one of the rules in my own personal code, one that I share with my close friends, is, "I will surround myself with people who ask more of me than I ask of myself." If you want to be successful, surround yourself with people who will push you up. Get rid of the others. Always be around people who demand more, who see more in you sometimes than you can see in yourself.

Another rule that I follow is "Don't compromise." I will stick with an issue until I feel it is completely resolved. I will not give up just to keep the peace. I stay with the issue until it feels resolved.

Whenever I have an upset and something goes wrong in my life, part of my code says, "Stick with the problem until you get the lesson behind it." My mentor Buckminster Fuller once said, "An upset is the opportunity to get to the truth." If you're upset about something, it means there's something in there to learn. Not somebody to blame, not some way to be a victim, but something to learn.

Sometimes that takes a while, and it's painful to face some of those hard truths about yourself. In the early eighties when I went through a very painful divorce, I spent a lot of time blaming my ex-wife, her family, where I was in my career and so forth. It got me absolutely nowhere. But when I looked back and really took a hard look at myself, I realized that inside me, there was a huge need to receive approval. As soon as I realized I was compromising all types of values in order to be liked, I realized I was doomed to repeat this process. The lesson was *inside* me. So I'll spend what some might call an "inordinate" amount of time looking within myself, trying to figure out how to stop generating the same problem or situation over and over again.

Finally, another example of one of my own personal rules is that I will always ask myself, "What is the next jump?" I need to always be learning. My Code of Honor says that if things are getting comfortable, it's time to jump to the next challenge. Some people may say I'm nuts, but I do know that I must keep learning. So when things start to get easy or to level off, when I find myself getting bored and find that I no longer have to try, I immediately know it's time for me to head to that next level, to get out of my comfort zone and move into something new. It's how I make sure that I'm continually challenging myself and being the best person I can possibly be.

In our family, one of our rules is, "There is no exit clause." That means that no matter how hot things get, nobody is going anywhere. There is no "out." We're committed to each other and the family and will stick with any problem that arises for as long as it takes to resolve it.

Another rule is that we "never go to bed in the middle of an argument." And sometimes that means we're up late dealing with it until it's resolved. When we've stayed up and pushed through it, those moments have been some of the most special, powerful moments in our relationship. Our code, though sometimes difficult and exhausting to follow, has made our marriage stronger and healthier.

We have other agreements and rules about how we deal with our kids. And the kids have a code, too. It gives everyone certainty and security in knowing what is expected and that we can trust one another impeccably. It doesn't restrict us, it brings us closer, creates more intimacy and love. Rest assured as well, our kids don't run around like little saluting soldiers. It is actually quite the opposite.

Team Tip:

Because we have these rules, very little negative stuff comes up. We are big enough to move past it. Because the kids have clear boundaries, they are very free to exert their creativity and energy inside those boundaries.

Remember, your code not only strengthens your team, it sends a message to the world about what you stand for.

These are some examples of my code just to get you started as you reflect on your own. It's time that you decide what's important to you and those around you. Your own personal code is a testimonial to who you are. What message are you sending? What will you *truly* adhere to and be willing to hold yourself accountable for? Because long after you're gone, people will remember more about what you stood for than what you earned.

Chapter Five

How to Enforce the Code to Ensure Championship Play

The truth is that lots of teams have rules. Some even claim to have a code. Yet the true test of rules is whether they are abided by and taken seriously. Enron had rules, Global Crossing had rules. Large accounting firms like Arthur Anderson have strict reporting rules. The issue isn't the rules, it's what happens when they are broken.

The challenge is enforcing them and making them stick. The big question is, what happens when someone breaches the code or breaks a rule? Do you punish him? Spank him? Give him another chance? Fine him? The truth is that many times nothing happens. People look the other way. They don't want to be seen as troublemakers or be cast out by the group. They certainly don't want someone to get even with them later for confronting them on something.

As a parent it can sometimes be more of an inconvenience for you to enforce the rules with your kids than it is for your kids, so in this case you let it slide. So what do you do?

"Call It"

You'd be surprised. The answer is really simple. If someone breaks a rule, you have to CALL IT! That's it? Yep. That's usually enough. Remember, the fear of public humiliation and ostracism by your peers or team is typically greater than the fear of death. (In a study I read from George Washington University, untimely death ranked number three on the list!) In most cases, simply calling an offender directly or as a team is confrontational enough. If people have a high level of certainty that they are going to be "called" on something, they will do most anything to avoid the embarrassment or rejection.

But here is the double-edged sword. The fear that causes "calling" to work is the same fear that intimidates you from doing the "calling." You see, your team's mettle is challenged after the code is created. The toughest part is calling it.

Team Tip:

Rules themselves are not the issue. Calling breaches of the rules early and consistently is the challenge.

Problems occur in many relationships in business, marriage and teams when people don't have the courage or the skills to confront each other with the truth. We don't want to hurt people's feelings and we don't want to face retribution. But a Code of Honor is absolutely useless unless people are willing to call it. In fact, every time the code gets enforced, it gets stronger, and consequently, the team gets stronger and the performance gets higher. If a rule gets breached, it takes the whole team down a notch if it's not called. It implies that you don't mean what you say. In other words, there is no honor.

Think about what happens with kids. If you don't enforce a rule with kids, they'll push it. You can say, "Don't torture your brother!" But if you don't enforce that, you'll be sending several messages: 1) that torturing your brother is really okay, 2) that rules don't matter (which is where criminal thinking and behavior come from) and 3) that rules are made to be broken. The same is true in any organization.

Look, rules are going to be breached, because we're all human. We make mistakes. Under pressure, we revert to our instinctive behavioral survival patterns. That's why you have a team and a code to support you in being the best that you can be even in the face of adversity, confusion and doubt. If the code is reinforced again and again, operating within the code becomes instinctive.

The bottom line is that you have to "call it" and it must be consistent.

As I mentioned earlier, it's not just the manager's or boss's job to call it. If you're going to have a great team, it's everyone's job to call it. And if everyone knows to expect that everyone is watching out for them, that's consistency. If you have ever played any kind of competitive sport, you know that if you are not pulling your weight, you won't have to wait for the coach to get on your case. Your teammates will be all over you! If it's left to a "higher authority," boss or manager to call it, you don't have a real team. You have a group of people working for somebody, but that is a far cry from a championship team!

On smaller teams, there is rarely need for fines, punishments or penalties. Larger or repeated breaches may obviously have to carry consequences, but at the first hint of an infraction, you just call it, cleanly, directly and early. The longer you wait the uglier it can be, and the tougher it is to muster up the guts to do it. Having to face someone, one on one, takes courage, commitment and strength: all the elements that you want for a great team. It's that kind of behavior that builds character on a team and in your family.

The bigger the team, or the larger the organization, the clearer the rules and consequences need to be. In those situations, you can't talk or communicate with everyone on the team all the time, so stronger controls may have to be put in place. Let me give you an example.

I spend a lot of time overseas. One particular country that I do quite a bit of work in is noted for having one of cleanest, most crime-free cities in the world, one of the highest standards of living and among the highest per capita GDPs in the world. It is also true that they have lots of rules and there are fines for just about everything, from carelessly dropping trash on the sidewalk to chewing gum! That's a lot of rules. One thing that they do that shows a clear understanding of calling it is that in the local newspaper, anyone who has broken one of those public rules gets their picture put in the paper with a description of what they did. How embarrassing! Yet, it works! (By the way, I am *not* an advocate of public humiliation.)

"Why so strict?

Because this country is a tiny island city-state with about 3 million people compressed into a very small area. In their desire to be an economic power, to support the economies of Asia and to be the beacon of commerce, enterprise and finance, the founding fathers felt that discipline would make them strong in a sea of chaotic development and challenge, particularly at the time when they became a nation.

As another example, I have a client who is the flagship airline for that same country whose code is very tight as well. That is why they boast one of the best safety records in the world and have been voted the best airline in nearly every category year after year. They absolutely will not tolerate anything less than the best, from the equipment, to the service, to the behavior of its staff. Breaches of the code are handled quickly, directly and very quietly.

The spirit of this airline is amazing. Those who work there are incredibly proud and work extremely hard. Why? Because they "call" something else as well. They post, publish and circulate the pictures and stories of staff members throughout the organization who get caught doing something *well*...who are actually caught upholding and strengthening the code.

For example, a staff person who offered personal services to provide local transport for a distressed passenger who missed his flight. Another team member who worked beyond normal shift hours and even helped to finance the reunification of a family separated by a terrible tragedy. A ground staff person at an overseas station who went above and beyond the call of duty to take a distraught family under her wing and offer her home as a sanctuary during a time of unrest while the family was attempting to leave the country.

These stories and pictures are circulated to every staff member around the world. There is even a series of hugely prestigious awards that are given each year to those who exemplify the code in this manner.

I study these situations because they are great examples of the principle that the tighter the code, the higher the performance, if you are willing to call it. (And remember, it doesn't always have to be a negative call!)

Yet be careful. There are obviously dangers of too many rules or rules that are too strict on your team or in any organization. Unenlightened leadership and misuse of rules and their enforcement can create abuse on *any* team. It can also put people in fear, which can totally kill innovative thinking, pride of ownership and resourcefulness. It's happened more than once. That is why on your team *everyone* must be able to call anyone without fear of retribution. The distinction on this one will become crystal clear in Chapter 7.

There are several reasons to call it. First of all, it heads off negative behavior that impedes performance. That's obvious. It also builds character, honor and pride by engendering a spirit of being willing to do what we agree to. It becomes something that binds the team together.

But there is another reason for calling it. What happens when there are rules in place, someone breaks them and no one says anything? In a little-known book called *Managing the Equity Factor* (written by Richard Huseman, Ph.D., and John Hatfield), the term used to refer to the results of unacknowledged rule breaking is "stamp collecting."

Stamp collecting rears its ugly head whenever people go underground with their gripes. It destroys teams from within like cancer, and it nearly always happens when nobody is willing to call it.

Let me explain.

I may be dating myself a bit here, but do you remember years ago when you'd go to the grocery store and buy groceries, and for x-amount of groceries they'd give you these little green stamps? You'd keep collecting them and would put them in a little book. And once the book filled up, you'd cash in the book for a prize.

The same thing happens on teams. I'll show you. Let's say you and I are on a team, and one of our team's rules is, "Be on time." Now I just *know* that you've never had to wait on anyone, and I'm sure you've always been on time for everything, right? Yeah, sure.

So let's say that we've agreed to a sales meeting time of 8:00 a.m. on Mondays. And then I show up five minutes late for our first meeting. The meeting's already begun, and I walk in five minutes late. What happens? Well, typically nothing happens, right? I sneak in, people sort of look around, the meeting goes on and *nobody* says anything about it. Somebody catches me up later, and that's it. Right? The problem with that is... at that very moment, subconsciously everybody collected a stamp.

You've collected a stamp when that "little voice" in your head says, "I thought we all agreed to be on time. I showed up on time. Now Blair shows up five minutes late, and nobody says a word! What's wrong with this picture?" Familiar with that one? I thought so. At that moment you just collected a stamp.

So let's fast-forward to the following week when I, or someone else, show up five minutes late *again!* And again, nobody calls it. And everybody collects another stamp for their book. And then next week, somebody else is a little bit late, and again nobody calls it. Stamp.

Chances are this isn't just a problem at the Monday morning sales meeting. People who have a hard time being on time usually have it in lots of areas.

So let's say this goes on for a while, and then there comes that one day when you're having the Monday-Morning-from-Hell. You can't get it together, you overslept, the kids are late for school, traffic's terrible, your significant other has said something that really irritated you and you're running late. You are frantically trying to get to this meeting on time and it's going to be close ... really close.

Suddenly a thought pops into your brain: "You know, Blair was late a bunch of times. Frank was late, Mary was late, and nobody ever said anything! And every time, I have busted my behind to get there. You know what? I'll just get there when I get there!" At that point, you just cashed in your book of stamps. That's when the F-18 starts to fall apart in midair. The team implodes or reverts to a cynical every-man-for-himself attitude. Stamps turn into covert actions to get even and sloppy behavior turns into poor results and nasty energy.

Teams don't need competitors to kill them, they do it to themselves. If you have a code, you have to be willing to risk momentary discomfort by calling it in order to reap the rewards of championship play later.

I agree it's not easy, and for sure they never taught you how to do this in school! They actually taught you to be quiet, be still and just do as you're told. So here are some guidelines and tips that will make calling it a simple and normal part of your team. If you follow these tips, it will get easier and easier until the fear and emotion disappear from the equation.

1. Pick the appropriate time to call it.

In front of a client or that person's peers is probably not the best time to do this. Humiliating a person will get you nowhere. Emotions will be high and he or she won't hear a word that you are saying. All that person will be thinking about is getting even. Remember, fear of public humiliation is greater than the fear of death! Not a good idea to trigger it if you're looking for a favorable response.

Calling it is not fighting. Attacking someone will force him to think only about defending himself, what his comeback will be and when his shot will be to get in *your* face in the future.

If it helps, take some time to cool off first, so that you don't come across as too aggressive. Use nonthreatening language and tonality. If your nostrils are flaring and the veins are bulging in your neck, I guarantee that the person you are calling ain't gonna hear you. A person who feels attacked isn't going to be reasonable with you and nothing will get resolved.

2. If you're uncomfortable, acknowledge those feelings first.

For example, you could say, "You know, I feel very uncomfortable talking to you about this. I've actually been upset about something since this morning, and I find it difficult to talk to you about it, but I'm going to give it a shot because I think it will help everyone."

This isn't about "blazing" anyone. Lead with your own personal fear, emotions and considerations in the beginning of the conversation. That way it releases a little emotion on your end, and it will typically soften the other person and make him more receptive to what you're saying.

3. Ask for permission to call it.

Ask him or her, "Is it okay to talk to you about this right now?" If he or she says, "Absolutely not, I'm too busy right now," then ask when *would* be a good time. Don't let the person put you off indefinitely, but at least ask permission.

4. Correct the behavior, not the person.

I'll say it again: Correct the behavior, not the person. Think about the really important people in your life, the ones you really care about. If you really wanted to, is there something you could say to each of them, about them personally, that would *completely* annihilate and devastate them? Yes, of course you could think of something. But you wouldn't.

That's what I'm talking about. Depersonalize it, and deal with the behavior, *not* the person. You can do this by referring to the behavior rather than the person. For example, "It seems that this idea of keeping time agreements has become a problem. I know that we all agreed to be on time, but you obviously are having a tough time with that one. What can we do to correct it?"

Team Tip:

Let the code legislate the behavior. The code gets to be the impartial third party, the policeman—not you!

Make lots of use of the word "we." You're appealing to the benefit of the team, rather than making it a personal issue.

And here's one of the magical things about a Code of Honor. You let *it* legislate the behavior, and you let *it* enforce itself. The code gets to be the impartial third party, the policeman. You can point to the code and say, "It's not me attacking you, it's what the code says. And you and I agreed to it." There's really nothing there to argue at that point, and you haven't attacked anyone personally. Saying, "Your whole miserable life doesn't work because you keep doing this," won't work, as you can probably figure out.

5. State specifically what didn't work and offer support.

Avoid "the whole story." Don't get into every detail about it. State what happened specifically.

For example, "We had an agreement to be on time for all the meetings, and you were twenty-five minutes late. It forced us all to wait. Do you need some support? Do you need to be reminded in advance of the meeting? Let me know, and I'll remind you so that we can all be on time next time." Quick, pure, simple—just get it done.

And offer to be supportive early in the conversation. When I was in the air freight business, we had a young fellow working with us who was a great customer service person but just could *not* get there on time. Everyone was always waiting around for him, covering for him. We told him over and over again to be on time. He wasn't trying to be disrespectful, but he just couldn't get it together. We told him that as much as we liked him, one more time and he would have to find another team to be on ... not ours. We discussed it at a team meeting and a couple of the warehouse guys piped up and said, "Don't worry, we'll take care of it."

The next morning, two big Samoans showed up at the fellow's apartment, knocked on his door and woke him up! They welcomed themselves into the house while one guy got him dressed and the other made the coffee. They did whatever it took to get this kid to work on time. And it worked! Now *that* was what I call "ruthless support"! And do you know that our friend cleaned up his act! He seemed to start taking things a bit more seriously, more responsibly, started dressing more professionally and definitely started coming to work on time. (The prospect of another wakeup call would be enough to get me out of bed for sure!) The team helped him to be the best he could be.

6. Make sure it's clear what the benefits are for correcting the behavior, not just for the team, but for the person being corrected.

What would be the benefit to that person in being on time? What would be the benefit to the team if everyone was able to operate according to the Code of Honor? Always take people to a "higher ground" of aspiration. Dealing with the minutiae of who did what and why and when will drive everyone nuts. Most people want to be the best that they can. They just need to be reminded sometimes.

7. Remind this person what he or she has already agreed to.

Remember, you all created these rules *in a sane* moment. You've already agreed to the standard. This person may have forgotten it in the heat of the moment. Remind him.

Allow the person to respond, hear him or her out without interruption or rebuttal, and say "thank you" for being willing to listen to you.

Acknowledge the behavior that you want.

Down the road, when the person *does* correct the behavior, acknowledge it. Thank him. You have no idea how powerful that is. Most people spend most of their lives without acknowledgment. If you're going to be a great teammate, a great leader or a great family member, sometimes you have to shut up the "little voice" in your brain and be big enough to simply say, "Well done!" Give him a high five, a pat on the back ... something to encourage that willingness to correct. It doesn't need to be a big deal. You don't need to make a big public announcement.

Team Checklist:

How to "call it":

1. Pick an appropriate time to make the call but don't wait too long.

2. Acknowledge how you are feeling first to the other party.

3. Get permission from him or her to make the call.

4. Correct the behavior, not the person. Let the code be the policeman.

5. State specifically what did not work and offer support.

6. Make clear what the benefits of correction are for the team and for the individual involved.

7. Thank the individual for listening and listen to his or her response without interruption.

8. Acknowledge the proper behavior later when you see it demonstrated by the individual.

What if You're Receiving the "Call"?

Taking correction is tough. But at some time or another, we're all going to blow it and make a mistake, or break a rule. We're human. So here are a couple of tips for how to take the correction if someone's calling you on something:

1. Take a deep breath.

Did you ever have someone come up to you, and you just *knew* that person was going to tell you how you screwed up on something?

Nobody likes it. But to be part of a great team, you've got to be willing to hear it. So the first rule is, take a deep breath. It seems corny, but what happens when people are confronted is that emotion goes up and breathing gets shallow. Sometimes a person will even turn pale. Taking a deep breath relaxes your body and oxygenates your brain so that you can think and listen clearly.

2. Acknowledge that whatever the speaker is saying is true for that person.

He or she may be completely off base, but at least understand that for that person, what's being said is important and true, and it took a lot of courage to bring it up. There may even be a lot of fear associated with saying this to you.

3. Listen actively.

Don't mentally check out and start building your defense, or a way to justify your actions. Just listen, and listen *all the way through.* My guess is that if you listen all the way through, you will find that you probably both agree on the point that this person's trying to present to you. But if you try to cut him or her off and prepare your defense ahead of time, you're never going to hear it.

4. If you made a mistake, admit it!

The minute you admit to the mistake, the discussion's over! We're done, we move on. It's only when people try to justify their actions with all the reasons why that you'll sit there all day talking about it. Probably the most powerful three words in the English language, and also the hardest words to say, are "I am sorry." It's very hard to say it and, in fact, many of us can't. There are some who would rather go to the grave being "right" in their minds rather than simply admitting their mistakes and being gracious enough to apologize. You probably know someone in your family who struggles with it. But if you can say that you're sorry, you will have done more to help the team than you know.

If you really have a hard time with this, here's a tip: Pretend you're somebody else. In other words, if someone's calling you on something, step outside yourself and pretend you're somebody else looking *at you*. It works for me a lot. I have to depersonalize it, take myself out of it, and say, "Yeah, Blair, you scumbag, you *were* late again! How come you do that, and what can we do to correct it?" I take it outside myself.

5. Ask the person how you can make it right and make amends to the team.

This is very important. Show that you care about the team, right away.

6. If the call that's being made isn't accurate (which is possible), simply go back to the Code of Honor.

Go to the specific rule or issue and get mutual clarity about what it really means, so that you can come back to an agreement.

7. Become truly interested and inquisitive about the call.

If you're truly concerned about holding this team, this marriage or this family together, when someone calls you on something, or even if you're calling somebody else on something, you will ask questions and make sure everyone involved really understands the call. Ask, "How might others be seeing my actions?" or, "Why would you come to that conclusion?" Start asking those kinds of questions, not out of cockiness or arrogance, but from the point of view of trying to understand where that person's coming from.

If you can do these things, or even if you can do a portion of these things, you'll find that your team becomes tighter and tighter and more committed to that set of values.

The Downside of High-Performance Teams

I would be remiss if I didn't tell you that having a Code of Honor didn't have repercussions. You see, the pendulum swings both ways. While stamp collecting happens if you *don't* call it, on the other side there will be some who may accuse you of being too "kamikaze" or "over the edge" about calling it. But the higher you want the performance of your team to be, the more direct the call has to be.

As a result there may be fallout. Some people don't like being accountable to others, or to themselves, for that matter. People will deselect themselves from the team. They may weed themselves out. They may even, consciously or unconsciously, push and test the boundaries to see if it's all for real. Just be patient and work through it.

Using the Code to Recruit Great Team Members

In all the businesses I have been in, we have used the code to interview new candidates. Assuming they had the basic qualifications that we mentioned earlier, the candidates would then sit down with someone on the team who would simply go through the code and give examples of what each item meant. Would-be team members then found out really quickly what it meant to work in the company and what behavior was expected. Lots of people considered us to be a bit weird, but you know what? Those who signed up were totally committed.

We have screened more people away through that process than anything. People *want* to do the right thing. People want to operate under a core set of values, but when they really understand the personal commitment, the personal sacrifice that it sometimes takes, and that they have to be willing to do those things, they say, "No, that's not for me, I'd rather go drive the '63 Chevy than fly the F-18. That's too much for me."

Team Tip:

The code is an awesome recruiting tool and qualifier.

You have to stick with the code, and you have to live by it. That means calling it. Get rid of stamps. Sometimes people will collect them, anyway. It's natural. Call that, too. Clear the air. Dealing straight with people empowers you. It builds confidence and makes you feel that there's nothing you can't do. You've conquered your biggest fears. That's a pretty great feeling.

Calling Yourself

In the final run, if you're attempting to pull a team together, once you've set this code of conduct, everyone has to lead. What does that mean? It means that if you breach the code or if your behavior goes out of line, as it will, since we are all human, you have to be willing to "call" yourself on it—to the rest of the team. Calling others is one thing, but the most powerful thing that a leader can do is to call him- or herself. If you do that publicly, in front of your team, your spouse, your kids, your peers or your staff, and say, "Yes, that's something we agreed to, and I blew it. I apologize, and here's how I'm going to correct it," people will take you seriously. If you're a big enough person and you feel strongly enough about these values and are able to say this, people will see you as a role model. And most important, they will learn from you about how to call themselves. You will at that point have made more of an impact on people than you will ever know, and everyone's performance will get higher. That makes you a great leader.

Team Drill:

1. Discuss what level of performance you want. Does every one agree? Make sure.

2. Cite examples of stamp collecting on your team and what effect it had on the team.

3. Practice or role play calling it in a controlled environment or at a team meeting. Follow the steps.

4. At your next team meeting call someone on *good* behavior or results.

5. If you have a current issue with someone that is a breach of the code, make an appointment with that person immediately to talk it through.

6. Decide as a team if it is okay to call things in front of the rest of the team.

Chapter Six

Leadership That Teaches Others How to Be Great

Leaders are judged by many criteria. By their impact, influence, accomplishments, reputation and so forth. Yet many simply leave it at that. Win-loss records don't occur by accident. Great accomplishments are not acts of magic. To create great families, businesses and teams, the great leaders have certain skills and talents. *I will also say that everyone leads in some area of their life.* You may never build a multi-billion-dollar business, but you may raise a super family that touches the lives of everyone they meet.

Here are some of those required skills.

Leadership Skill 1: *The Ability to Spot the Strengths in Others, and Get Them to Play to Those Strengths*

One of Woody Hayes's biggest strengths was also one of his downfalls. As a leader he could quickly and accurately assess an athlete's strengths and weaknesses. He was great at putting the right player in the right position. That's why he recruited such great teams.

He and John Wooden, the legendary coach from UCLA basketball dynasties, shared the same belief. You can be a great coach, but if you don't have the talent on your team, you still won't win the championship.

To be a great leader in business, understand that everyone has a God-given strength of some kind. That is why everyone has the ability to succeed. It's your job to spot it and build on it.

For most of our lives we are told our strengths and weaknesses through batteries of performance reviews, tests and evaluations. The most common feedback given by those who administer those evaluations is to "fix" your weaknesses. Marcus Buckingham, author of the bestseller *First Break All the Rules,* points out that it's hard enough trying to figure out what you're naturally good at, let alone trying to change something that's probably hardwired into your brain. Wouldn't you agree?

That's the point of *SalesDogs.* You don't have to be an "attack dog" to be successful in life! Different people are different breeds, with different strengths. A great leader helps you find that strength and then helps you develop it and capitalize on it. He or she doesn't try to pound a square peg into a round hole.

The highest-paid athletes are very good at what they do. Their gift is the physical prowess they possess. It's unique to them. A great coach spots that specialty, that thing the athlete's *great* at, and then encourages him or her to focus on developing that. A well- designed team has few redundancies because everyone is playing to their unique abilities and not trying to perform functions that are a struggle to them.

A leader's talent is knowing all the positions that need to be played and recognizing who is best suited to play them. Then he coaches his players into that zone of discovery, experimentation and implementation. As a parent our job is to do that with our kids: not to make them into what we wanted to be or what we were, but to find what the strength is in them.

As a parent and a leader, you can inspire that in yourself and others. You know why? Because we love to work on stuff that we're already good at. Right? It's hard work, but it's fun. Time slips away and before you know it, you've been working on it for hours. Struggle is replaced by excitement. Distraction is replaced by focus and intensity. Recall those times when you have become lost in time doing something that for others would seem tedious or hard, but to you was exciting.

Tiger Woods obviously has a great talent for golf. I once saw him in an interview with Oprah Winfrey, and she asked him whether his talent allowed him an unfair advantage over others because he wouldn't have to try as hard. Tiger gave her a look of bewilderment.

He said, "No, it's actually the opposite. It's almost a curse. Because I have the talent I feel obligated to be great at it. That's why I think my greatest asset is that I practice more than anyone to develop that talent!"

Now, a friend of mine grew up playing golf in southern California at the same time Tiger did. They're the same age, and they played the same courses. My friend told me that everyone used to *hate* Tiger because he was so slow in getting around the course! That's because he analyzed, experimented, assessed and scrutinized each stroke to the nth degree. It drove everyone who played with him nuts, and the group behind him wasn't really happy with him either. But did he care? Obviously not, and it's a good thing! Now my friend pays to play golf, while Tiger's getting paid to play. That ought to tell you something.

Leadership Skill 2: *The Ability to Teach*

One of the biggest secrets to success in business, which only a few people know about, actually goes beyond selling. It's the secret of being able to *teach* others.

The ultimate form of leadership is the ability to teach your team how to be successful—not by telling them, or by reciting a monologue on how to do something, or by telling them what you did, but by getting them involved, practicing, drilling, challenging them and getting them dirty in the process.

You don't learn to play ball by just watching game films. You don't learn to raise kids just by doing what your parents did. You don't learn to build a business from a book and you certainly don't learn to be a great team player by being told how to do it. You have to be *taught* how to do it.

It's no wonder that we miss this very important point. It goes back to the idea of conditioning. Our impressions of learning and teaching are based on our experiences in school. What happened in school wasn't necessarily teaching. How much of it do you actually remember and use? I had a handful of wonderful teachers who really *taught* me, but most of them were professional "tellers."

Teaching is a combination of leading, selling, motivating and involving. It's the delivery process of education, which comes from the root word *educate,* which means "bringing out or drawing out" the intelligence in others. Education, therefore, does not mean to cram data down someone's throat! Be a teacher and a leader, not a preacher!

Education, or learning, is the practice of repetition and discovery. For example, the more you experience the act of selling, by repeating it and drilling it, the more you discover how it works, how to apply it and how to get rich.

At Ohio State, lots of All-American players came back to be assistant coaches. Very few of them actually became head coaches anywhere else. It's because they could play and show, but they couldn't teach and lead. Big difference.

We had an expression on the team: "Once a showboat, always a showboat." In other words, some people want to be a star. There's nothing wrong with that. But that has nothing to do with being a great teacher. It's not about showing off your own competence and brilliance. It's about getting everyone on the team to be great, helping them learn something that will make *them* great. That's why, with a few notable exceptions, you don't usually see a lot of professional sports coaches who were also mega-superstar athletes. It's just a different skill and mindset.

The secret for getting people to learn isn't having the knowledge, it's teaching people how to learn.

Which brings me to the next leadership element...

Leadership Skill 3: *Using Mistakes to Empower and Strengthen the Team*

A great leader knows how to use mistakes to empower the team, while those who don't can use them to kill a team. This is because our conditioning has taught us that mistakes are a bad thing. We have a natural distaste for them. School taught us that. We were penalized for, and embarrassed by mistakes and in many cases were made to look stupid because of them.

Coach Hayes was good at spotting strengths, but also could spot a weakness just as well. Later in his career, he spent so much time focusing on trying to correct weaknesses that it became his downfall. I remember in my senior year we went to the Rose Bowl for an unprecedented third straight year to play the University of Southern California. He told the team before that game that the only way we would lose would be if we made mistakes.

As a matter of fact, he was so obsessed with eliminating mistakes that he instilled the fear of making any into the hearts of the players. He would rant and rave about it, scream and scold, jump on his glasses, rip up his hat or shirt and even resort to pushing and punching when mistakes were made in practice.

Sometimes fear can be a great motivator, but in business and in sports it can also be destructive if handled improperly. If you're constantly thinking to yourself, "What if I blow it?" or, "I'm not sure if I can do this," then as soon as a mistake *does* occur (and it always does), then you automatically tell yourself, "See, I told you."

At that point you proceed into a downward spiral that I call *panic*. Fear and emotions go up, while intelligence and competence go down.

A great leader understands that dynamic and teaches his team how to deal with the emotion, by drilling the ability to successfully respond to mistakes. A leader teaches how to take fear and convert it into power and high intention.

In that Rose Bowl game, we went into the game favored to win by several touchdowns. Yet we fell prey to the very fear the coach had. The fear of making mistakes became overpowering, which ironically caused the team to make more mistakes.

We ended up losing by a score of 18-17. It was a heartbreaker. We didn't lose because we lacked great talent, and it wasn't because we didn't have a plan or the skills to execute it. We lost because the team had been conditioned to fear mistakes at such a level that it became almost fated that we would lose for that very reason.

Look at your team, organization or family. There are probably those who are afraid to fail. If the fear is strong enough, it will become reality.

Are these same people focused on winning, or afraid of failing? There's a big difference between the two.

As a leader, knowing how to spot those mindsets, and how to coach them, is critical to building a great winning organization. What are you communicating to them, through your actions and your words? What happens when your child comes home with a bad report card?

In business, you're going to make mistakes. If you teach your team to expect them, how to learn from them, and even how to laugh at them, you will be giving them a lifelong skill that will make them winners, no matter what. If you can do this with your kids, they will grow up to be strategic risk takers and great problem solvers.

Team Tip:

There are three ways to use mistakes to strengthen the team:

- Debriefing
- Celebrating wins
- Knowing how and when to call a time-out

---

1. Debriefing.

The key to learning from mistakes is asking the right questions. Debriefing a situation teaches someone how to look at any situation as a learning experience, not as a tragedy. As a leader, it isn't about correcting, advising, lecturing or even consoling. It's about asking good questions. It's about getting people to understand what happened and to take responsibility for learning something as a result of the experience. Use these five questions for debriefing any situation:

1. **What happened?** We only want facts here, not opinions.

2. **What worked?** Keep this brief and opinion-free, if possible.

3. **What didn't work?** Notice the language here. It's neither right nor wrong. It either works or it doesn't. You have to answer both of these questions, because they always coexist.

4. **What did you learn? (This is the most important question!)** Look for patterns of behavior or results, not a single isolated incident.

5. **What can you do to correct it (if it was a mistake) or leverage (if it was a win)?** You have to answer this question last. Otherwise you may put something into action that could create more problems than you had to begin with.

Correcting a special-case scenario isn't productive to the process. For example, say a hotel front desk worker is faced with an irate customer, who complains about his or her experience in the hotel. The desk worker has no previous record of run-ins with customers, and when the customer leaves, so does the problem. That's not a scenario that needs a policy change.

However, if the desk worker starts getting complaints or having run-ins with customers every other night, you know you have a problem at the front desk. That's a situation in which question 5 plays a part.

This whole sequence can take seconds, minutes or hours. But once this becomes a ritual, it will force accountability and quick correction and it will leave emotion out of the process. It's perfect for team meetings, or questioning behavior that is not in line with the code. Most important, it keeps people from taking it personally.

It's amazing how quickly the negative energy and fear come off mistake making through debriefing. In any situation, it puts the ball in the court of the person or persons who were involved in the error or the success. It ensures accountability and allows them to discover answers and strategies for themselves. Energy goes up, risk taking accelerates and mistakes are actually minimized. Sometimes you have to bite your tongue to keep from just telling them what to do, but trust me—let them learn for themselves. Coach and teach, don't tell.

Debriefing puts responsibility on the team members. Don't do this in a condescending way. You're simply asking questions and being honest. And through it, the person will *own* the mistake, without feeling like a moron. As Bucky Fuller once said, "If you assume the person is smart, they turn out to be brilliant." If you expect people to succeed and learn from their mistakes, they will.

2. Celebrating all wins.

One of the most important things you can do as a leader is to teach your team how to celebrate even the smallest of wins. It reinforces winning activity.

I'm not talking about schmoozing your team here. I'm talking about complimenting them on a job well done. And it's got to be sincere. You do it for your kids when they're little to encourage, acknowledge and support the behavior that you want. And it works! Their energy is high, they love to win, they love you for it—and for some reason we don't do that with anyone else.

Instead, we start thinking, "It's expected," "It's your job anyway," or back to that stamp collecting mentality, "When was the last time they celebrated one of *my* wins?"

Appreciation and acknowledgment of the efforts of another human being is one of the most powerful gifts you can give to someone. In fact, a battery of case studies conducted by Harvard University on compensation programs and financial reward systems discovered that money did far less to encourage long-term peak performance than a simple show of appreciation. In the organizations that I've coached over the years, it's the single most powerful, yet most difficult culture change to make in any organization. Try a simple handshake, high five, pat on the back or "thank you," coupled with a lot of consistency, and you'll be amazed at the energy and results you see.

3. Calling a time-out.

Another technique is one that you can observe in any NBA playoff game where the score is close. It takes fifteen minutes or longer to play the last two minutes of a game. Why?

Because the teams are always calling a "time-out." They are regrouping, re-strategizing, debriefing and doing their best to shift momentum so that they increase their odds of winning, or if for no other reason, then to snap players out of a negative downward spiral.

Knowing when to call a time-out is a hugely valuable skill. With your team, with your family, with the significant others in your life, you have to know when to call a time-out. Otherwise energy drops, emotion goes up and relationships can be severely damaged.

Most organizations and teams, when I ask them if they debrief experiences, say yes, but that they call it a "post-mortem." A phrase that means "after *death*" being used to describe what is essentially a learning process! The connotations of that are negative, and imply also that it's done after the situation is over, and it's too late to correct anything. But if you take a time-out, and regroup *during* the game or high-pressure situation, you have an opportunity to succeed at *that* project—not just the next one!

Just take a few minutes. If everyone's emotions are ruling crucial decisions, the decisions could be poor. And if you are a leader, others will follow your example. Better to call a time-out—which does not have to be a long one, either. At the first sign of confusion, disappointment, anger, sadness or apathy, *stop,* and call the time-out. You will be amazed at how much you can get cleared up early and how high the energy you can sustain if you're observant enough to nip problems in the bud.

And by the way, you don't have to know how to "fix" everything as a leader. That's a trap. Most people can figure out solutions if you simply stop the clock for a minute, allow the pressure to subside a bit and let the emotion drop. Then people will think clearly and once again become their brilliant, capable selves!

This brings me back to another quality that exists in great leaders . . .

Leadership Skill 4: *Creating and Maintaining Frequency of Interaction*

Maintaining frequency of interaction with your team builds trust-preferably actual contact, one on one, either in person or by phone. Without it, people wander off. They forget what all the work is for, they lose track of the mission. We're human, and we need human contact. People and names become real, not just labels on an organizational chart. Processes become human and the spirit and passion of the team becomes something you feel, not something that is a bullet point on a PowerPoint presentation.

This is especially true for families. That's why many families have a ritual Sunday night dinner. It's one time when everyone in the family can touch base, get to know each other again and "recharge" their batteries. My father always insists that our family have a reunion every year. And every year I fight it. But you know, it works. We all enjoy it, and it helps us all to remain close.

Don't rely on e-mail. That's too easy. There are people who will say things in an e-mail that they would never say to someone in person. Ever get an e-mail with an attitude attached? If something is important and you want commitment, make the commitment yourself to contact your teammate directly. You will be amazed. They can conveniently "lose" or misplace an e-mail, but they can't deny your conversation.

You wouldn't send a football team out to play a game without having practiced. So why would you expect a team to achieve peak performance without having frequent interaction? Whether it's a short meeting, a retreat, a conference call or merely a lunch, maintaining contact is crucial for the success of any team.

Leadership Skill 5: *Ability to See and Communicate the Brightness and Possibilities of the Future*

No, I'm not talking about being a psychic. I'm talking about being able to see the "big picture" and knowing what the win will be for your team and the individuals who are a part of it. What is the overall goal? People need to know what their incentive is for working hard and giving their all.

Every team ought to have long-term and short-term goals. Achieving both on a regular basis gives everyone an opportunity to celebrate wins often. Every great leader knows that people have the potential to become their best under pressure and adversity. But getting through it sometimes feels impossible. What is that light at the end of the tunnel that will get the team to push through? Answering that question is the challenge of a leader.

The great leaders in history had this ability. Martin Luther King, Jr., did this better than most. His "dream" or vision of the future still compels people around the world today. In his own words:

"I have a dream that one day this nation will rise up and live out the true meaning of its creed: 'We hold these truths to be self-evident, that all men are created equal.' I have a dream that one day on the red hills of Georgia the sons of former slaves and the sons of former slave owners will be able to sit down together at the table of brotherhood...I have a dream that my four little children will one day live in a nation where they will not be judged by the color of their skin but by the content of their character."

Even on the eve of his death, he still held that vision. He said:

"Like anybody I would like to live a long life. Longevity has its place. But I am not concerned about that now. I just want to do God's will. And He's allowed me to go up to the mountain. And I've looked over . . . and I've seen the promised land. I may not get there with you, but I want you to know tonight that we as a people will get to the promised land. So I'm happy tonight, I'm not worried about anything. I'm not fearing any man. Mine eyes have seen the Glory of the coming of the Lord!"

King knew that offering such a brightness in the future would bring out the best in people. He and other leaders like him inspired others to be their best by encouraging them to endure pressure and adversity, because only through that would people learn, grow and realize greatness.

Don't get me wrong, leadership doesn't mean you have to be Martin Luther King, Jr. But a great leader leads by example. A great leader is a person who is willing to face challenges, address breaches and encounter hardship in order to live up to their and the team's potential.

A leader has the skills of communication, persuasion and sales. Martin Luther King, Jr., John F. Kennedy, Gandhi, Eleanor Roosevelt, and other great leaders of history sold dreams and visions to millions. Leadership is selling others on being the best that they can be. John F. Kennedy once said, while giving a speech about the space program:

> "But why, some say, the moon? Why choose this as our goal? And they may well ask, why climb the highest mountain? Why, thirty-five years ago, fly the Atlantic? Why does Rice play Texas? We choose to go to the moon. We choose to go to the moon in this decade and do the other things, not because they are easy, but because they are hard! Because *that goal* will serve to organize and measure the best of our energies and skills. Because that challenge is one that we are willing to accept, one we are unwilling to postpone and one we in tend to win, and the others, too.:"

Kennedy challenged the American public with a mission that would be difficult. He said that it would bring out the best in all of us. Don't you want to do the same with your team? Your kids? Your staff? Yourself?;

Leadership Skill 6: *Ability to Sell*

One thing you will also notice is that every great leader in business, politics, sports or families can sell. Sales is not just selling to customers. It's compelling vendors, lenders, investors, staff, regulators to support your team. It's also about you selling you to yourself to build the confidence and courage you need to lead. In *Sales Dogs* I maintain that everyone can sell. It's about selling a vision, selling an attitude, selling the code or just selling ideas to the team. They have to also sell the team's work or efforts to other teams and other authorities. You become the spokesperson for the team. Typically those who sell the best end up running the organization. The most important form of leadership in sales is selling others on themselves, giving them more confidence, power and spirit.

Champions of the Code

Finally, when it comes to the Code of Honor, the highest form of leadership is having the willingness to call yourself when you know that you have breached the code. You have heard it before. You have to walk the walk, not just talk the talk. Practice what you preach. Lead by example. It all boils down to the fact that if you have the courage to do this, others will take you seriously and will be inspired by your humility and strength. Showing vulnerability and accountability publicly shows incredible leadership. The fear of embarrassment, however, keeps most politicians, business leaders and individuals from ever exercising this very important power.

A leader must become a champion of the code, and his greatest demonstration of this will be when he can call himself. A leader isn't the policeman of the code, but he supports it wholeheartedly. Because if a leader is going to lead a team into a difficult and uncertain future, that team is going to rely on that code to legislate when things get tough. Without it, people will resort to their own codes, which may not serve anyone else but themselves.

Leadership Checklist:

Work on your ability to:

1. Spot and leverage the strengths of others.

2. Teach others how to succeed.

3. Use mistakes to strengthen and grow the team.

4. Use frequency of interaction to build relationship, consistency and most of all trust.

5. Promote a realistic but bright future to the team.

6. Sell.

Everyone Can Be a Leader

I assert that everyone can lead and that everyone leads at some time or another in life. Not everyone can lead a multinational corporation, and not everyone can lead a family of five. But in our respective worlds we all have the opportunity to lead. There have been hundreds of books written on leadership. There are "level-5 leaders," servant leaders, charismatic leaders, and so forth. Some push from behind, pull from the front, inspire from the middle ... I could go on.

I subscribe to what I call "the Roulette Wheel of Leadership." Sooner or later the ball drops on your number and you have the chance to offer direction, inspiration, support, education or advice. One hopes that will happen more than once. It's whether you have the courage in that moment to step up and lead that matters. You may not follow any "popular" descriptions of what a leader is, but you lead nonetheless.

We were all born with natural gifts. And in this lifetime it is our job to discover and deliver them. When that happens, you will lead. Not because you want to, but because it's natural for you to do what you are best at. When that happens, others will follow you to learn.

In order to establish a great team, you have to lead. You may not be the designated leader, or maybe you are. Either way, you have to sell your ideas, teach others how to improve and rally your team. In this chapter, you've seen that you don't have to be Lee Iacocca to lead. You don't need to coach an NFL team. And you don't have to be superhuman to learn or use leadership skills. But every time you use them, you'll be leading.

Team Leadership Drill:

1. Listen to great speeches of great leaders. Listen to their words, strategies and motivations. Model the strategies that will work for you.

2. Practice the "debrief" model at all opportunities. Teach it to others. Make note of the shift in accountability.

3. Find simple ways to acknowledge wins, without great fanfare but with good energy. Use high fives, handshakes and so forth. Practice them sincerely without trying to schmooze.

4. Call at least two time-outs this next week and check in with the team.

Chapter Seven

The Biggest Impact of the Code

There are several reasons for having a Code of Honor. As I have said, one reason is to set the standards of behavior and conduct for the team. The higher the performance desired, the tighter the rules. The code takes the arbitrariness out of what is expected. It also is called a Code of "Honor" because it consists of rules that we all take seriously, that we commit to and that we hold ourselves accountable to. In other words, we walk our talk. It becomes our badge of honor.

The second reason for a code has even greater scope and consequence. The reason that a team, a family, an organization, a culture or a nation has a code is that the actions of its members have an impact on the lives of others. That's right. Regardless of what you think, your individual actions affect the lives of other people, directly and indirectly. No one acts in complete isolation. Your adherence to your standards and rules, as well as your breaches of them, ripples out to others around you.

As a simple example, take a rule like, "Be on time." What are the consequences of your being five minutes late? Is that so catastrophic? Well, maybe not, but the real issue is that you have now affected the time and energy of fifteen other people who were waiting for you for five minutes. Not only is that nonproductive, but in essence you just stole over an hour from others who consider their time to be precious to them. And even if they weren't physically waiting for you, the "little voices" in their brains were saying, "What's going on with Blair? Is he committed to this or what?

Did he forget? I wish everyone would play by the same rules," and so forth. And that is a waste of good mental energy!

Let's say one of my personal rules is "Deal direct," meaning that if I have a problem with someone, I deal directly with that person to resolve it. That would mean no gossip, no backstabbing and no disparaging remarks about that person to other people. But let's say that I have some tension with my brother-in-law that I don't deal with. I may tell myself that the only people it really affects are myself and perhaps him. But that's not true. Because I have now affected my wife's relationship with her brother, my kids' relationship with perhaps their favorite uncle, and then their relationship with his kids ... you see what I mean?

This also happens in nearly every business team that doesn't deal directly with its issues. It affects productivity, creates tension and causes others to feel they have to step on eggshells so as not to create upset when warring parties are present or when unresolved issues are lingering in space. That is a waste of energy.

Everything you do somehow affects those around you. Never doubt the importance of creating and upholding your own rules.

You're sending a message of what you feel is important. As you or your team ultimately achieve power and success, others will look to you as an example.

Sports creates classic examples of this. Imagine the week before a major college football game, the star of the team somehow compromises the team's code two nights before the big game. There is a ton on the line. The coach has to make a decision. Does he let his star player play and look the other way? Or does he enforce the team rules and force him to sit out? The pressure is high. The media, sportswriters and fans are having a field day with the controversy.

It comes game day. Two teams of great talent line up to start the game. The coach, after deliberation, decides to play his star. Which team has the edge? You guessed it. The other team. For the first half of the game our player in question performs horribly. Not only that, his team is out of sync, for some strange reason. When the smoke clears they have lost the game. But they have lost more than the game. They have lost their honor.

The coach had an opportunity to make a statement, to show leadership and character building. But he succumbed to the pressure of winning at all costs. He did not think about the repercussions of that decision on others. Instead he sent a message that rules aren't that important. That if you are a star, you can get away with making up your own rules. It created friction for the team, threw them off track and tarnished the reputation of a great program and coach.

Losing the game was only one outcome. What about the thousands of young, aspiring athletes who look to college players as role models? What message was sent? That if you're a star, you are above the rules? As you can see, I could go on and on, but the bottom line is that the decision to not support the rules affected many more lives than those on the playing field that day.

You can find examples like this in sports, business, entertainment and politics. The question is, how do your decisions and particularly your adherence or non-adherence to the code affect others?

This brings up another important part of the Code of Honor. The code is a statement of who you are as a team, family or individual. Each decision that you make does in some way affect others either positively or negatively. The code not only polices the team, but ensures a positive impact on the community, the marketplace and all living things, either directly or indirectly.

For a new or small business, this is critical. The statement you make by your team's actions positions you in the market. If you hold to high standards internally, but treat vendors, associates and others poorly or dishonestly, you will not survive long. The code that you create for your team must also be the code that you use in the market place.

If you profess to hold your business to certain standards, yet allow those standards to be compromised, you have sent several messages to the market: that you are not true to your word, that you can't be trusted and that certain folks are "above the rules."

More important, if enough businesses do not play by their own rules, it tells the whole market that rules aren't important. The problem with that is that what goes around, comes around. If rules are breached by you, they may be ultimately breached by others against you. It becomes a precedent in the marketplace.

The United States was founded upon a strong Code of Honor. It's called the Declaration of Independence and subsequently the Constitution. The Founding Fathers signed that document upon the threat of losing their lives. As a nation we have a strong code, as many nations do, but what happens when those rules are breached by the very folks who are elected to defend and support them?

Look, we all mess up. I can honestly say that I don't walk on water and I have had times in my life when I have screwed up big. Like any of us, I have taken shortcuts, gone back on my word and certainly have not felt good about those instances. Yet, it is part of my code to either call myself on that behavior, be willing to be called on it or somehow come clean on it.

The highest form of leadership is being willing to publicly call yourself on breaches of the rules and apologize. Voter turnout in America is among the worst in the world because many have lost faith in their politicians. Not that all politicians are bad. But unfortunately, those few who've screwed up and broken the codes have broken more than the rules. They have broken our trust.

Trust is created by being true to your word. My point here is that when you breach the Code of Honor, and particularly when you don't clean it up directly, you breach the trust of your team and other teams that interact with you. You may be sending a message that you are undependable. Earning trust takes time, consistency and making good on your word and actions. Once trust is broken, it's extremely difficult to win back.

In the case of most corporate scandals, it isn't an issue of having a code or rules, it's whether the rules were followed or whether breaches of those codes were ever called. We think to ourselves, "If they'll cheat on their financials, where else will they cheat?"

Some people would call that ethics. Ethics is an emotionally charged word. I would prefer to simply make the point that you can measure the value and power of a decision or action by observing the number of people, businesses and communities that are positively or negatively affected by it. This is critical not only to the success of your business, but to your reputation.

The more groups that are benefited, the better the action or decision. In the case of that football game, the coach's decision to play his star player seemed to benefit him and the athlete himself. Yet it negatively affected the team, the program, the university and young fans. That's why the code is there. To ensure that under pressure we do what is best for the most in the long run.

Unfortunately, I can cite lots of sports examples where breaches of a team's code resulted in a negative impact on the team's performance. I can also cite examples of great coaches who have turned failing franchises into winning teams by implementing and enforcing simple practice rules and personal rules of conduct where there were none, while using the same personnel.

Every decision that you make within a team, and even for yourself, has ripple effects. What are the ripples? The more groups and teams and individuals that are benefited, inspired and motivated by the decision, the more positive the decision is.

Team Tip:

You can measure the value and power of a decision by observing the number of people, businesses and communities that are positively or negatively affected by it. This is critical not only to the success of your business, but to your reputation.

You have to ask yourself if your company policies and actions benefit your company but harm others. The more groups your decision negatively affects, the less support you will receive in return. If you treat vendors unfairly in order to enhance your own profitability, reputable vendors will not want to deal with you. You may even create resentment and revenge from arenas that you never expected.

On the other hand, the more individuals, groups and entities that are supported, honored and advantaged by you, the more the market and community will reward you. If your business supports positive community efforts, sponsors educational endeavors or makes an effort to truly give back to the community, you will attract other businesses and clientele that support as well.

A company builds a manufacturing plant. It creates more jobs. Good. It increases profitability, which benefits shareholders. Good. But it treats its staff poorly and staff turnover is high. It has run-ins with the environmental protective agencies because of questionable operational practices. A company like this faces a questionable future if it doesn't clean up its act.

Have you ever seen individuals or businesses that seemed to be successful, but had a reputation for generating success on the backs of others or at the expense of others? What ultimately happens to them? Check the records.

Your rules have to take other factors besides profitability into consideration if you are committed to long-term sustainability. If you say you are going to operate fairly and with respect toward others, that had better be with everyone, not just your customers.

For example, there are companies such as J.M. Smucker & Co., which was recently rated as one of the "Best Companies to Work For" by *Fortune* magazine. Its corporate culture includes objectives like, "Listen with your full attention, look for the good in others, have a sense of humor, and say thank you for a job well done."

Businesses like this have a code that is designed not only to achieve peak performance and profitability, but also to treat its own team members in a way that makes them feel that they are winning too. They know that it is good for business.

There are successful companies like Ben & Jerry's Ice Cream, which from its very beginning in 1978 devoted over 7 percent of its pretax profits to foundations that empower other nonprofit organizations. It had product lines that committed part of their revenue streams to protecting the environment. And even though the company is now owned by Unilever, it still maintains the practice of giving back to local communities, championing environmental issues and treating its staff as family.

At Rich Dad, the CASHFLOW for Kids game is given away for free to any school or educational institution in the country that wants to support its youth in obtaining financial literacy.

The list goes on of great companies that make a conscious decision to make sure that all parties are advantaged by their business practices, policies and profits. Their rules apply to everyone they touch directly or indirectly. The list includes those companies that people love to work for, those that volunteer in various ways to support their local communities and those that commit money to assist a variety of important public issues, foundations and causes.

What is interesting is that most of these great companies that make the "Best of whatever. . ." lists have these values and rules written right into their codes. It's who they are.

The code is designed to protect its members from detrimental treatment and behavior. It is also designed to protect and advantage others outside the team as well. The great and enduring institutions of the world perpetuate themselves through the consistency of their Codes of Honor. This is true of nations, religions, multinational corporations and the small auto repair shop around the corner. However, if breaches of and inconsistencies in those rules begin to seep through, doubt, cynicism and lack of respect emerge. I am sure that you can cite your own examples.

So how can you do this with your team?

When you set up your policies, rules and code, make a conscious decision to make sure that the business, the team, the suppliers and the customers win. But if you want to experience the unparalleled support of rabid fans, make sure that your community wins too. I know that it seems hokey, but the best companies do their best to give back to the communities from which they take. The bigger your game, the bigger your support.

The same is true of great families. If you tell your kids not to lie, but then you cheat on your taxes, or fail to uphold a promise you made to them, they learn from your actions and may perpetuate that attitude with others. Your actions had better send the right message.

We had many rules growing up that I didn't understand at the time. Many of them seemed like a burden, and I rebelled against them continually. But they were sending a message. It was a message of how to, as my grandparents said to me, "Do the best by others." It was a guiding principle that took my grandfather from poverty to wealth. It permeated every business decision. It was a message that has helped guide me in my business and in my life and has empowered thousands of other businesses.

What message are you instilling within your family, your business, your team or yourself? What is the code? Whoever you are, your code has an impact on others—your vendors, your customers, your community, your entire marketplace. We get so wrapped up in making the decisions that are right for our team, or our business, that we sometimes forget how our behavior affects others.

Your code has to be enforced not only for your benefit, but for that of countless others whom you touch, directly or not. It's your reputation, it's your legacy, it's a statement about how big a game you play and how many people you touch. The more you touch positively, the more you will be benefited.

Team Drill:

Review your rules.

1. How many different entities are benefited by those rules?

2. Look in your community. Are there businesses or individuals that seem to be successful but have a reputation for achieving success at the expense of others? What have been the repercussions?

3. How do you want others to look at your business?

4. Discuss examples of organizations that create positive ripple effects on many others.

5. What message do your rules send to others who associate with you?

Chapter Eight

Ensuring Accountability, Loyalty and Trust

In essence, when you create your code, you are setting standards of behavior and performance for yourself and your team. Therefore, you have to decide how high the standards are going to be. Are you going to walk a mile a week, or run a mile a day? How tight do you want your code to be? How high will your performance be? Do you want to drive an F-18 or a Chevy Nova?

Rules and standards are useless unless people are willing to be accountable to them. The simplest way to keep everyone accountable is to have them keep track of their activities and results in a quantifiable manner—in other words, keep track of their statistics. I'll explain.

People always ask me what the single most important motivator in sales is. I usually laugh and tell them that it's the Monday morning sales meeting. They look at me strangely, since they are usually expecting some slick strategy, tactic or technique to come rolling out of my mouth. But it's much simpler than that.

When I first started learning to sell at Burroughs years ago, we had an 8:00 a.m. sales meeting every Monday. There were no fiery speeches, incentive program announcements, guest speakers, training or anything.

All it consisted of was taking your prospect sheet and posting it on the wall, then going through each prospect in front of the group. You'd have to explain the status of each prospect, what stage of the sale each was in, how long until you were going to close those deals and what it would take to make it happen. You also had to announce to the group how much you were going to sell that week, and where and how you were going to dig up more qualified leads.

God help the person who had the same prospect up there more than a couple of weeks in a row. You'd get booed and hissed out of the room. I swear that the sales activity was highest on Thursdays and Fridays because nobody wanted to show up at that Monday morning meeting with old prospects or the same set of lame strategies.

It wasn't even about the money. The prospect of public humiliation (remember, fear is numero uno) is what motivated us. And it worked! Why? It's called accountability.

It's being answerable for results and agreements that you make. Now, I'm not a big advocate of complete and total public humiliation, yet what makes a team and its players number one is accountability. Are you willing to be answerable for results, both good and bad? Are you committed to learning, to your health, to your family, to your friends and to your team? Are you able to make good on your promises and projections, and to be responsible for your successes, mistakes and failings?

I've never met a great athlete or a great businessperson who wasn't accountable at some level. Once you are willing to set standards and hold yourself and others accountable to them, the level of play increases. That's what happens when you enforce the code.

So why wouldn't people want to be accountable? Well, because sometimes it's hard. Nobody wants to look at themselves in the mirror and admit that they didn't live up to expectations, or that they possibly fell short. The easiest way to avoid failure is to never set yourself up to fail. And the easiest way to do that is by not setting standards and certainly not holding yourself accountable. With no accountability, you don't have to ever look in the mirror!

If I tell myself I want to lose weight, but I can't drag my lazy butt to the gym, it's a lot easier to blame my stressful schedule and all the people who expect things from me than to just admit I've been lazy. Right? Accountability can be uncomfortable, embarrassing and difficult, but it can also make you feel proud and accomplished. Yet, if you know that I'm not even accountable to myself, would you want me on your team?

Greatness at all levels is bred out of accountability. As a parent, spouse, business owner, leader, teammate or friend, honestly looking at your actions and holding yourself accountable to them determines the quality and standards of your life. The code spells them out. Calling and being called on them gives you the opportunity to improve and move forward.

In sports you are held accountable by the coach, other teammates, the fans and your statistics. The numbers don't lie. You either made calls or you didn't. You either ran a mile or you didn't, you either kept your agreements or you didn't. And great players know before anyone else does if they need to be called on something or not.

Loyalty comes from respect. Respect comes from being accountable. Accountability comes from a commitment to the team, the code and calling it.

There are a few ways to ensure accountability, commitment and loyalty on your team.

Statistics

Each member of the team has got to keep statistics on results and measurable activities. From one week to the next, that's how you measure your strengths and weaknesses. No stats, no results!

What do I mean by stats? A network marketing client of mine has a Code of Honor rule that states that team members will share their appointment books with the others on the team on a weekly basis. This way they can show activity levels—who they're meeting with, how often, how many people they're calling on—it keeps them accountable to the team. They set targets for their different activities and then they log in their actual numbers. It's very revealing and somewhat uncomfortable, but it allows support and growth.

Team Tip:

Accountability is in the "Stats"! No "Stats," no results!

So let's say that one person on the team sets a goal that she will make a hundred new calls every week, and she will make five - presentations. If her team looks at her activities and discovers that every week she's exceeding her goal for calls, but falling short in presentations, there may be a problem with how she's calling on people. It then becomes much easier for her to be coached on to success.

Keeping statistics also reveals wins that ought to be celebrated, such as achieving more than the agreed-upon goal. It also reveals where potential problems may be, such as in the area of converting initial contacts into live presentations. It also allows you to see patterns over time.

Sometimes trying to change behavior patterns is like watching grass grow. Slow and dull, right? We feel like it's taking forever and nothing's happening, and then what do we do? We beat ourselves up if something hasn't changed over a very short period of time, or we change strategies before the current one has had time to play out.

Think about your last plan to lose weight. You worked out at the gym every day, you cut back on sweets, you ate salads for dinner—and you weighed yourself every day, hoping to see change. You kicked yourself for that one cookie you ate if your weight hadn't dropped. But if you give it some time, and watch what happens each week, charting your behavior every day, then you may look back in six months and realize you lost a few pounds and a percentage of body fat, right? Maybe you will even realize that over time your energy has gone up, or because you can now observe your own patterns you notice that you tend to eat when you're under stress. It teaches you a lot about yourself. That's what I'm talking about.

If you keep stats, you can observe patterns, measure progress and solve problems. Without them, you get discouraged, you won't be acknowledging your wins and most important, you will have forgotten how far you've come. Looking back six months, you'll never remember what you ate, how much and when.

The key is not just keeping final numbers. It's measuring the activities. Did you change your approach? Did you have help? What was going on that day? Tracking your activities allows you to see your behavior and your progress, or lack of it. It also allows you to be coached properly.

A true team supports each other unconditionally. This is not about being shamed into action. That's why many people are afraid of accountability and of being on a great team. They're afraid of being scrutinized. That's just the "little voice" in your brain that's been conditioned to think that feedback is personal, painful and harmful. The more feedback you get, the easier it is to take. If you avoid it like the plague, each rare time that you get it, it's going to be tougher and tougher until you avoid it altogether.

Team Tip:

The more feedback you accept, the easier it gets to receive it!

This is about being supported and encouraged by a team that has your best interests in mind. In one of the organizations that I work with, the idea of coupling accountability with a game resulted in the creation of a "fantasy football" game, in which people are put on teams where they receive points for sales activity and practice. These points are gathered in a software program where the teams compete in playoffs to see what team can score the most points. This simple model surged activity levels by over 400 percent!

People were motivated by fellow team members in two ways. First, if they weren't up to speed, other members jumped in to support immediately, since they all had something to win in the end.

Second, no one wanted to let down their teammates, so they pushed extra hard to "earn the right" to be considered a great team player. The dynamics of this were incredible.

Without accountability, there is little to measure your progress or the progress of others. But then again, it comes back to knowing who's on your team. You don't win a championship unless you're willing to be held accountable. Statistics make this very simple. The late Dr. Edwards Deming, the guru of quality management, said it simply: "If you can measure it, you can improve it." This is true in manufacturing as well as in human behavior and performance.

It doesn't always mean that you will succeed. Nobody does all of the time. But if you're willing to put yourself on the line, magic happens. Numbers go up, more people show up and your income increases. That's why, to be successful, you need a team. A team will call you on your breaches of accountability. They will also high five you on your accomplishments.

Becoming Committed to a Team

A mentor of mine said something that became part of my own personal code. He said that one of the keys to mastery is surrounding yourself with those who ask more of you than you do.

Do you have friends who give you a boost when you need it, who are willing to give you a push when you falter and even kick you in the behind when you start letting yourself and others down? Surrounding yourself with those kinds of teammates is the fastest way to change your life, and your stats.

As a team member, you have to know the team's got your back. Calling each other is the highest form of accountability. By entering into the "contract" of a Code of Honor, you're making a commitment to each other that you won't let yourself or your team down, and you'll do what it takes, no matter what, so that the team can accomplish its mission successfully.

Ask yourself how committed *you* and your team are to each other. People these days are always jumping from one team to another, from one job to another to find a "better situation," a better salary, a better opportunity—but they don't realize that without sticking with something and becoming committed wholeheartedly to it, they won't improve, and neither will the team. It's important to find that out.

When I got my first job in sales, I made a commitment to myself that I would stick with it for three to five years, no matter what. I wanted to learn to sell, and I knew that if I didn't really give myself that chance, I'd never know what I could have gotten out of it, or how successful I could have been. Sure, there were better products and better commission plans, but it wasn't about that. It was about building discipline without distractions, being able to "stand in the heat" of any challenge that would come my way and simply squeezing the most value I could from the training, experience and mentorship that was available.

You have to demand the behavior you want for yourself. You also have to demand it of others, otherwise you are left holding the bag. I am sure you know what that is like. Why in the world would you demand less of others than you demand of yourself? That is being cheap, and even treasonous, to you and the team. If someone breaches a commitment he or she has made to the team, it's got to be called. And when someone is living up to a commitment, you have to acknowledge it. If you do that, the energy goes up, commitment goes up, performance and speed go up, and it gets really fun.

Loyalty

When I talk about Codes of Honor, enforcing codes, being accountable and making commitments, some people respond with, "Why does it have to be so hard? It sounds like you're trying to run everything like a football team, or the military!"

That is not what I am talking about. The truth is that when the boundaries are tight, it makes it much safer to bounce all over the place inside those boundaries. People feel free to speak their minds, be crazy, think out of the box, celebrate wins, acknowledge and thank each other and be honest with each other. And when those things happen, it creates an air of electricity, fun and passion.

In that environment, trust abounds. You really get to feel that everyone else has you covered and that there is no legitimate favor that won't get acknowledgment.

It also breeds loyalty and the willingness to be there for each other, to resist the temptation of going for more tantalizing opportunities at the expense of others.

If you don't have loyalty with your friends or your teammates, demand it. And above all, demand loyalty of yourself. Be loyal to your word and be loyal to those important people in your life. Set examples that send a message about who you are.

If you as a parent tell your eight-year-old that you will be home at 5:00 p.m. to play basketball with him, but you decide that it would be more fun to stop at the pub on the way home for a few beers, where is your loyalty? What are you telling him? What has your eight-year-old just learned about you and about loyalty?

In the workplace, people tend to take care of themselves first, as I've said before. Many Codes of Honor have a rule that says, "Be loyal to the team." It's a great rule, but what does it really mean?

Let's say you have a customer service representative handling a complaint from a customer on the phone, over one of the company's policies. Perhaps that customer service rep feels she's being loyal to the customer when she says to them, "I know, you're right, and that's what I told them [the company], but they never listen to me. I'm sorry, I did what I could." When that customer hangs up the phone, what do you think that person is thinking? The customer service person was trying to be "nice," but what she did was stab the team in the back in that attempt. The customer is probably thinking, "Boy, that place is really messed up. Their own people are turning on each other!"

Stand united with your team. Don't hang your team's dirty laundry for all to see. That's not what loyalty's all about. Even if you disagree with the system, a rule or a policy, you remain loyal to it until things change from within. That's not to say that you shut your mouth, follow blindly and disregard your feelings. But you fight for change internally. No freelancing or going out on your own. You work *with* the team, not against it. If you don't do that, nobody wins.

Remember, the whole reason for all of this is that in moments of pressure and high emotion, intelligence is low. When a team is under stress, when the chips are down, do they remain loyal? Some people would help a stranger before they'd help a family member. Maybe you know someone in your own family like this. But that's not a great relationship, and no real team would behave this way. That decays a team from within.

Acknowledge the heck out of loyalty in the face of temptation. And if you don't get loyalty, demand it. It's easy these days to be disloyal to a team if you find a better offer somewhere else. But I'll tell you, it warms my heart when someone tells me he or she has stayed put because they feel a sense of loyalty. That brings a team together. And if that happens on my team, there is *nothing* I won't do for that person.

Watch great football teams, at the end of the fourth quarter when it's fourth down and long, and there's little time left on the clock. In the huddle, they'll hold hands. They've got each other's backs, no matter what. Now that's what a great team is all about.

All we really have in the end is our relationships. They might as well be the best.

In the final analysis, just follow these simple rules to ensure accountability, commitment and loyalty:

Team Checklist:

1. Make sure you have statistics and that you review them, learn from them and leverage them.

2. Acknowledge the behavior you want.

3. Get permission to hold each other accountable and be supportive in the process.

4. Choose your teammates and your friends wisely. Surround yourself with those who will demand the best of you and themselves.

5. Demand loyalty and resist temptations to wander or seek better options.

6. Be accountable to yourself and set the example you want.

7. When in doubt, support each other.

Team Drill:

1. Identify measurable activities that lead to the results that you want for the team.

2. Keep statistics on those activities and review them with the team weekly.

3. Have all members of the team do the same for themselves.

4. Create a forum that allows team members to hold each other accountable for their "stats" and be supported.

Chapter Nine

Standing in the Heat with the Code

I am sure that you have heard it before. Greatness is born out of adversity. Unfortunately that isn't true in all cases. Under pressure and adversity, many times emotion climbs, and we don't always emerge as successfully as we'd like. It can be ecstatic and it can be ugly. The reason for a code is to hold everyone together under pressure, to ensure that everyone will be disciplined enough to stay committed and strong when the challenge arises. Every great team, great person or great family that I have ever seen became that way because of pressure. It's like John F. Kennedy said: "We choose to go to the moon ... not because it's easy but because it's hard!" True transformation happens only under pressure and challenge. There is a certain physics to it. A weird predictability. Most of all it brings out the best in us if we hold together "in the heat."

For all of us as individuals, situations of intense pressure, stress or challenge cause us to change. Sometimes it's for the better, and sometimes not. Typically, those situations heighten our emotions, sometimes depleting our ability to think rationally. That's when instinct and the survival mode kick in. For some it's fight or flight. For others it's withdraw and run for cover. For some it's "CYA." For others it's courage, bravery, brilliance and strength. What's the difference? The code.

The Code of Honor, if it's securely in place, holds things together. Through enough commitment, practice and repetition, it overrides old survival instincts and holds things together. It forces us to stick it out, ride out the pressure and come out the other side stronger. I call this "standing in the heat."

My life has been about standing in the heat for as long as I can remember—not because I'm brave, but because at heart I'm a coward. I have found myself in very bizarre and difficult situations mostly because I had backed my way into them, or because initially they "seemed like good ideas at the time." Sound familiar? Don't get me wrong, I have a loving family, and I wasn't an abused or abandoned kid. I was just a person who always wanted something a bit better than what I had.

It seems there was always a pattern to my growth that was at first disturbing. As I began to make a life's work of studying successful people and successful teams, I found that pattern to recur in those instances, too. Currently, as a business owner, teacher, consultant and spouse, I have found that the greatest, most profound and permanent results have come from standing in the heat. And many of the ills and tragedies in our daily lives are a result of avoiding the heat, or of avoiding the difficult things that we know we need to do.

More important, as I have spent my life studying this phenomenon, I have come to find that pressure is not only how we grow as human beings, but also a fundamental law of nature!

Team Tip:

All great teams become great by taking on challenge, adversity and pressure and seeing themselves through it together.

The evidence of this comes from a Nobel Prize that was awarded in 1977 to a fellow named Ilya Prigogine. He was a chemist who studied the Second Law of Thermodynamics. Don't worry, this isn't a science lesson. I'll illustrate with a simple example:

If a tree falls in the forest and lies on the ground, over time it will rot and decay. Ultimately, it will fall apart, and its structure will erode into more disorder, or chaos. In other words, the Second Law says that if left alone, things in our universe slip into more and more disorder—they tend to fall apart. Make sense? See, already you're an expert on the Second Law of Thermodynamics.

Did you ever know a person who did nothing but sit all day on the couch watching TV while his or her life fell apart? We've seen organizations like that, that got fat, happy and complacent, and didn't seem to respond to competitive threats. They ultimately fell apart or faced ultimate collapse. The same can be said for countries, economies, currencies and cultures of all kinds.

Certainly our own relationships with our families and friends, if left unattended for very long, seem to decay and fall apart. This is the Second Law at work. It's true in nature and true in life. Physicists, chemists and sociologists have known this fact for years. Life cycles of companies were predicated on this law of nature. People over the years have resigned themselves to the fact that sooner or later things will "wind down," both in relationships and in our lives.

But Prigogine got his Nobel Prize for a different observation. His theory, in fact, seemed to be the opposite. He said that nature creates order out of chaos. He observed that if you take a normal organism or a chemical compound, and pass energy into it, it will take the energy in and pass it out. Much like ourselves: We take a normal daily allotment of work, food, conversation, challenge and input, manipulate it and pass it out in the form of energy, output, results, waste and the like. We all know this. But when we start adding *more* energy, overloading it and putting it under pressure, *that's* when something interesting begins to happen. In physics they call this "perturbation." Ever had too much on your plate? Ever been given one too many problems to deal with? Has your spouse ever unloaded on you one too many times? Were you *perturbed*? Catch my drift? Perturbation simply means upsetting the status quo.

Team Tip:

Perturbation simply means upsetting the status quo. That's where greatness comes from.

Prigogine observed that increasing the amount of energy in a given system begins to overload it until it starts to quiver and vibrate. And as the pressure and perturbation increase, it vibrates even more until it reaches a point where it seems that it can't handle any more. Just like when you've had a day where you were under such stress that if someone gave you one more thing to do you would scream! We've all been there. Whether it's you or a simple chemical compound, a large organization or a global economy, you've been perturbed "to the max," and have reached an imaginary threshold. You're truly "in the heat." It feels like you're going to explode. It looks like the organization is going to collapse. But in the right conditions, something else happens. And that's what Prigogine got the Nobel Prize for.

When a system reaches this pressurized threshold, *under the right conditions* (I repeat—the right conditions) something interesting happens. It doesn't fall apart. It doesn't blow up. It crosses the line. It actually *reorders* and *evolves* into a more complex structure that is able to handle more pressure.

Take our tree, for example. If it falls in the forest, into a bog, and sinks into earth, then under the pressure of the earth, over time, it turns into coal. Under even more pressure and heat, this same set of compounds ultimately turns into a diamond—a substance that is much more complex and stronger by far, and able to handle incredible amounts of pressure.

So what in the world am I saying? What is the point of this little science lesson? Well, what I'm saying is that in nature, transformation and growth occur under pressure, by *upsetting* the status quo and overloading existing situations. This is what happens to us!

Have you ever tried working out? As you pump your muscles, they feel like they're going to explode, like they can't handle any more pressure, but instead they grow and develop. You become more fit, and more able to handle weight, distance and pressure. But this only happens when the "heat" is applied—pressure. It's the way nature works, but for some reason we humans tend to avoid it, and run from the process.

Have you ever noticed, while perhaps you and your team were under a ton of pressure, working late and stressed to the max, that all of a sudden somebody said something and you all started laughing uncontrollably? And you had no idea what you were laughing about? Once you all calmed down, everything seemed easier, faster and smoother. That was the perturbation process at work. Pressure went up, emotion released—reordered!

You are standing at the top of a double-black diamond run, about to ski down. Your heart is in your throat. You can hear it pounding. You start down the hill and slowly but surely the months of practice and drilling start kicking in. You let out a wild scream as you jump into the next incredible turn and a few minutes later you look up and see that you have just traversed an incredible slope, more capable, more able to handle bigger challenges.

You've looked at scores of properties, run numbers for days, your spouse has been arguing with you about it the whole time. You have questioned yourself. You are stressed. But you sign the offer anyway and suddenly you are in your first deal! Had you backed off from the heat in any of those cases, the emotion that was holding you back would have lingered on and built until you became resentful, angry or cynical.

Nature wants you to go for it. That's how you evolve and how those around you evolve, too. Those friends who tell you to kick back and take it easy are giving you advice that is counter-evolutionary! The more you stand in the heat, the bigger you become and the closer you come to fulfilling your destiny.

Team Tip:

Nature wants you to go for it!

In an old study I read, I learned that retired executives who did not set a new and challenging game for themselves upon retirement had a life expectancy of about five years! If you aren't going for it, you aren't evolving and the second law of entropic disorder takes over. Your purpose in life is to grow.

Now I've told thousands of people about this idea, and they all agree that they'd like to grow, evolve, become fitter and more able. So I ask them why, when it looks like they have to face up to uncomfortable realities about relationships, finances, career and health, they do not cross that "imaginary threshold" and transform themselves and their relationships? That's what great athletes do. They push harder and harder until they cross the barrier into world-class status. Why don't we "average humans" do it? Why do 50 percent of the marriages in America end in divorce? Why, when the heat goes up, do we run for cover?

I'll go back to science again to explain. In this reaction I discussed earlier, there's something else that happens. As the system that is under pressure begins to transform, it releases energy. Usually, in chemistry, this energy is in the form of heat. As the system reorders, some of the bonding mechanisms release as the system evolves to a more efficient state. Now when humans release energy, it's usually in the form of—yep, you guessed it—*emotions*'. Anger, fear, sadness, confusion, frustration—all emotions you associate with pressure. And the reason most people avoid the heat is that they're terrified of the ensuing emotions.

As a society, we're not taught how to deal with emotion, work with it or even use it. Instead, we're conditioned to run from it, stuff it, hide it, deny it and scorn it. We grow up hearing things like, "Big boys don't cry!" or "Women should be polite." I'm sure you've heard it all. The problem is that if you don't allow the emotions to release, it's like stuffing the reaction. The process stops right there. When it comes to emotion, the typical reaction is, "How unprofessional," "That guy's a wimp," and so forth.

But the problem is that we're under pressure *all the time!* As our world gets more and more complex, we, our kids and our teams have more to deal with than ever before, and if the associated emotion isn't dealt with, sooner or later it will blow on its own. I'm sure you've seen people walking around like volcanoes, ready to explode at any moment. Have you ever said something to someone and nearly gotten your head taken off for no reason? Or have you ever done that to someone else? I bet you have. Like a Coke bottle, when you shake us up enough, we blow.

You see it in organizations, too. They're under a tremendous amount of pressure. Those that have avenues to communicate and release the confusion and anxiety continue to grow. Those that stuff it implode. The first sign of it is employee turnover. That's when people quit and leave. The brightest minds start leaving an organization because they feel abused or unheard and have no way to express themselves. Meanwhile, those who can discuss, process, or even "laugh" their way through it, as I pointed out earlier, can get through it. Releasing those emotions eases the tension and directs energy into pushing through the heat to the breakthrough at the other side.

That's why you have a code.

It is designed to protect the players in the heat of the battle. It legislates responsibility, communication, fair play, integrity and respect. What makes it work is the agreement to "call" behavior at the first outset. It allows you to communicate, vent and even be frustrated if you need to be, but not at the expense of others. Without it, even the best-intentioned people find themselves in a free-for-all. The code is designed to hold you together under pressure so that as a team or a family you can cross that line of transformation together.

Team Tip:

The code holds your team together under pressure and protects all its members when things get crazy.

Learning to stand in the heat is critical if you want to grow. But trying to do it without a code is like jumping with no parachute! You have to have a code for yourself, your team and your family so that you will support each other in times of need. That's what I mean about the "right" conditions. The context, the code and the rules must support, protect and nurture. If the rules and enforcement are abusive, laden with fear and demeaning, people will either never step up to the line or will become abusive and threatening themselves.

Have you ever noticed that once you've successfully dealt with a big problem, others like it don't seem so tough anymore? That's the beauty of standing in the heat. Once you cross the threshold, you have moved to a new level of being. You are bigger, fitter, more capable, able to take on larger tasks that were daunting before. But if you never cross the line, two things happen. First, you become a victim of the Second Law. What the laws of physics say is that if you don't add pressure, if you don't stand in the heat and go for it, the Second Law wins. You will degenerate in your career, your relationships and your growth. Reordering and transformation only happen under pressure.

Second, if you don't find ways to release emotion, you will keep storing up pressure until you can't hold it any longer, and you will blow. Degeneration, anger and explosion. It can show up as intense depression, violence or withdrawal. This can happen to our kids, our staff or even in our most important relationships if not managed.

Businesses can become so thick, impersonal and bureaucratic that they decay from within.

As I've said all along, I've never seen a great team become a great team unless it was under pressure. I've never seen a great accomplishment, great leader, revolutionary action or the like occur unless there was pressure. Great championship teams are not a big happy camp. They're tough because they push you, they make demands of you to always face challenges and be better. They hold you accountable for mistakes. But they also, if they're truly great, celebrate each other's wins. They learn from each other. They support and encourage each other. And together they accomplish far more than any of them would have believed. And in the end, they are satisfied, and they're better people. It's hard work, but it's worth it.

So how do you stand in the heat?

Well, if you've taken the steps in this book, and created a Code of Honor, you've begun the process already. Because as important as pressure can be in creating a great team, its members have to get through those rough spots, and their natural inclination may be to run, to avoid the issues. You need a set of rules, a code, to lean on. When the heat rises and everyone's looking around at each other, wondering what to do and how to handle it, the code will give the answer.

I have a Code of Honor for me because I am my own worst enemy sometimes.

Because under pressure, I forget, I get upset and I want to fight or run. Neither action serves me. I have been blessed in my life to be surrounded by teammates who hold me accountable. I have disciplined myself to stick to the code. I can tell you that I go through tough times like anyone else, but I have learned to trust the process. Whenever pressure gets high, when things seem to be going nuts, I tell myself, "I'm in the heat now. Just hang in there. Keep persisting." And you know what? Something great always pops out of the heat. There are days when I go ranting and raving around the office or the house and my wife will look at me and smile and say, "Well, it looks like something good is about to happen."

Whether it was learning to ski, buying my first rental house, building my businesses, running a race or simply coming to an understanding with my wife, there has sometimes been fear, frustration and confusion. But processing those feelings and standing in the heat under the protection of the Code of Honor has turned all those experiences into huge wins and has brought success and love into my life.

One of the rules at home and in the business is to never abandon tough issues or leave them unresolved. Sometimes that isn't easy. It feels like it would be easier to just let tough decisions or confrontational issues slide. Sometimes it can even get emotional. Yet it seems that when we allow the feelings and emotions to responsibly air and release, we not only find great solutions but, just as it happens in physics, we reorder to even greater levels in our relationships. This definitely happens with my business team, but most important, it has brought deeper and stronger connections at home.

In the business, we have nearly always emerged with a better idea, a new insight or a breakthrough in thinking. As strange as it may seem, my staff has actually come to look forward to those times of impasse, knowing that something great is just on the other side. This happens because we have made it safe for them to voice concerns, frustrations and ideas as long as they play by the code in the process. It has to be handled responsibly. No blaming, whining or wimping in the face of pressure.

When the stakeholders of any enterprise are willing to stick with the tough issues until they come to resolution, great synergy can happen. The issues may be finance, sales, partnerships, visions, goals, results, strategies, hiring, firing and so forth. I am sure that you have experienced your own tough but critical issues. New alternatives can get created. Higher levels of trust can be forged while commitment between the parties gets stronger. Yet none of that happens unless there is an agreement to stand in the heat until it's resolved.

I have witnessed this breakthrough in thinking, creativity and results in nearly every leadership program that I have conducted for clients around the world. In the programs themselves, I watch in awe as the participants struggle with some of the tasks and projects that I give them. I purposely turn up the heat by giving them a seemingly unrealistic amount of time and limiting their resources. In every case, those teams that argue, push, debate and tell the truth about their points of view have always popped through and produced project results that even exceeded their expectations of what they thought possible.

I was waiting for a flight in Austin, Texas, a few months back. A young woman approached me and could tell from the puzzled look on my face that I did not recognize her. She smiled and said, "You don't remember me, do you, Blair?" I shook my head. She went on to say, "I was part of one of the first leadership programs that you conducted here at IBM a few years ago and I want to thank you!"

At that point I remembered. Her team had struggled to execute a project that I had given them. They slaved late into the night pulling out their hair simply trying to figure out what project they could do and how to complete it by the following morning. There were times when they were not very happy campers!

I said, "Why are you thanking me?" She again smiled and said, "We pulled off that project, as you remember, right?" I nodded. She said, "Well that project has lived on and taken a life of its own over the years."

Their task was to create a project that would have sustainability beyond the program, but had to be completed overnight. It had to benefit the greater Austin community. Not just IBM or their team. What they created was a project to educate, serve and protect "latchkey kids" who go home from school alone to empty homes. It was such a resounding success that the local press writers wrote it up and it spread across the country, with all kinds of organizations taking on sponsorship of it.

She said, "I hated you when you gave us the assignment. I thought it was unrealistic and impossible. Yet when I saw what we accomplished by standing in the heat together as a team, the results were incredible. I have been promoted many times here at IBM over the last few years. I attribute a lot of it to that day. Whenever I face a challenge that seems impossible, I remember what we accomplished. I have taken on a mindset that *NOTHING is impossible.* It has always blown away everyone that I have ever worked with."

We spoke for a while and then I boarded my plane. As we climbed above the clouds and jetted into the reddening evening sky, I got a little emotional inside. How many children's and families' lives were affected by that team's willingness to stand in the heat? How have the lives and relationships of those team members changed and grown as a result? What if they had just said, "It's too tough, we give up"?

How many times have I doubted myself and felt that I was pushing too hard, asking too much of my staff, my friends, my clients and myself? Yet the laws of physics work for us, too, as long as there is a code in place that honors and protects the team and holds it together under pressure.

Jim Collins describes the gut-wrenching discussions and issues of companies like Scott Paper, Wells Fargo and Eckerd Drugs that had to make tough decisions to go from "Good to Great" in his book by the same name. He said it was their willingness to deal with the "brutal truth" that helped make them great.

Those who give up on issues or feel they're too uncomfortable to deal with end up having to deal with those issues sooner or later. The longer you delay dealing with them, the bigger they get and the tougher they are to resolve. It's like stuffing things into a closet and slamming the door shut instead of properly putting them away. If you keep doing that, sooner or later you open that door and you have an avalanche. And no one can stop an avalanche.

We also have a rule in our company and at home that everyone must commit to regular personal development training, from communication courses to personal counseling. By doing this, everyone works on themselves so they can be emotionally stronger and become better communicators. This is a huge discipline that has allowed everyone on the Rich Dad team to grow and prosper. It has also allowed my wife, Eileen, and me to grow immensely.

Look, you can't go around venting emotions on everybody. I certainly don't advocate putting down this book and screaming at your staff, persecuting your children or starting a fight with your spouse. That may be your instinct, but it won't solve anything. So what the code does is legislate your behavior. It says that even though you want to run, you can't. Even though you want to scream and dump all your emotions on a colleague or a family member, you can't. It allows you to speak the truth, to force accountability without doing it at the expense of others.

The rules say so, and way back when, before emotions were ruling your head, you agreed to it. Trust yourself and the rules, stick it out, and see the code as the thing that will keep you firmly planted in the heat. If you deal with the situation, you break through it, and you will be transformed. That's what the Code of Honor is all about.

Team Checklist:

Three keys for achieving greatness:

1. Pressure builds great teams in all arenas. Embrace it and don't run from it.

2. Find constructive ways to release stored emotion so that the evolutionary process can proceed—exercise, sports, discussion, whatever works.

3. Use the code to hold the team together under pressure. More than ever, if you stick by it in the heat, you will emerge more powerful, with better results and with a sense of incredible pride and accomplishment.

Team Drill:

1. Describe moments of high pressure and how they were handled—well or not so well. How could they have been handled better knowing what you know now?

Conclusion

It's Time for You to Have a Code of Honor

Well, here you are. One thing that I know about you, if you have come this far, is that you are committed to being the best. After all, if you can't be the best, why bother at all? Inside you and everyone around you is greatness. In some cases greatness is waiting to be revealed. Your task is to find it, train it, develop it and use it as a tool to better your life and the lives around you. Don't wait any longer. Take a look at yourself and the most important teams in your life and decide whether you're getting the most out of them.

My challenge to you is this: Ask yourself how much joy you want to have in a relationship. How much performance could there be lying dormant in your team that hasn't yet been revealed? When will the day come that you can look at yourself in the mirror and know that you are exercising all the potential you have inside? What are you willing to settle for or what are you willing to demand? What are you compromising on today and what would you be willing to stretch for? If, God forbid, you got hit by a bus tomorrow, how would you be remembered? What example are you setting? The quality of your answers to these questions determines the quality of your life.

Your Code of Honor will make a statement about you and where you stand. Wear it like a badge of honor, and let it guide you through the challenging times in your life to the breakthroughs and wins on the other side. If you can do that, the pressure and strife will transform you and your team into better people. And in the end, you will be able to look back without regret and say you had fun. That's what this is all about.

Think of it as a big game! Games have players, rules, boundaries, opponents, goals and even spectators. They're meant to test the best of you and your team. If you aren't celebrating wins, hanging out with people you like, learning, growing and laughing, stop now! Either do something else or change the way you're playing the game. You were meant to be happy! Not miserable or frustrated. Each person has a gift and the name of the game is to get everyone to do what he or she does best! Play the game with others who want to have fun on that journey with you.

The final judge of your team is this: If the entire game changed tomorrow, would you choose the same players? If the answer is yes, you just may have a championship team. Building a Code of Honor will nurture it, protect it and bring out the best in everyone. You *can* have the team that you want, the relationships that you want and the family you want. I want you to be the outrageously successful person you are meant to be. When you do it, it will be because you made a conscious decision to do it and created a context, a Code of Honor to make it happen.

So congratulations! Thank you for being willing to commit to your own Code of Honor, to being willing to set the standards and tolerances as high as you possibly can. And from here on out, never compromise on those values. Decide today who you want **to be!**

I began this book by telling the story of one of the greatest games in college football—the Ohio State Buckeyes playing the Miami Hurricanes for the national championship in the Fiesta Bowl. Even as the underdogs, OSU came back to win in a dramatic double-overtime game. The team's head coach, Jim Tressel, had taken over a program at Ohio State that was loosely disciplined and he instilled a Code of Honor that was tough but fair.

Throughout the season, his team had battled back to win from what seemed like certain defeats again and again in what appeared to be a season of miracle after miracle. Well, miracles happen. But they happen because you set them up to happen. Tight curfews, tight academic standards, rules of public conduct, training rules, singing the school's alma mater with the marching band, walking arm in arm in the end zone before each game and telling players who breached the code to sit out, or even to leave—all of these became rules that the team lived by.

In a speech that he reportedly gave to his team minutes before the kickoff, the power of the code, and of what it takes to build a championship team in your life, are clear. More than that, you can feel their spirit. You can also see why they won.

Imagine yourself in that locker room with eighty thousand roaring fans waiting outside and millions watching on TV every day you take to your own playing field, and whether you know it or not there are loving fans waiting for you to win, too. I will let his words echo in your mind the way they have in mine. May they remind you that you are a champion and give you the strength and motivation to take the most special people in your life and make them the best. I'll leave you with his words:

"Tonight, you embark upon the last portion of a journey that you started many months ago. Part of the journey involved some of our friends leaving us for various reasons to go their separate ways. But those of you who remain are a part of something special here. You stayed for a reason. You stayed on because you care about this team, what it stands for, your teammates and yourselves!

There comes a point in each person's life when he asks himself: How do I *want* to be remembered?

The reality is that so few people have the chance that you have tonight. You have the chance to affect the answer to that question. The moment is at hand. It's not about tomorrow. It isn't about yesterday. It's not about what you did ten minutes ago. But part of your future and how you'll be remembered will be shaped by *you* over the next three and a half hours.

Look around this room and look at the person next to you. How do you want that person to remember you? How do you want them to remember the way you played in this game? How do you want your parents, family and friends to remember your performance on this night? Will you be remembered as ordinary or extraordinary?

The coaches have prepared you for this game. You've prepared yourselves for this game. But there are several things to remember when you take the field:

1. Play with heart. No matter what happens, we don't let up!

2. Play with passion. Don't take this situation for granted. Although you earned the right to be here, don't assume you'll be back. Play it as if it were your last hurrah. Play every single play like it's the play that will save the game! As the game goes on, each play adds up to a winning performance.

3. Play within yourselves. Remember what you've been taught and play within that. So often, teams lose games because people start playing outside what they've been asked to do. Trust your mates and know they have your back.

4. Don't let anyone take this moment away from you. Not the crowd, not the press, not your friends and certainly not the other team.

5. Have fun! Relish this moment. An awful lot of young people will go through life wondering what it would have been like to be in your shoes. Enjoy this! Don't be afraid to win!

6. Play like *champions* tonight! Play with the champion's heart, mind, spirit and attitude.

All season long we've talked about what it takes to be considered truly extraordinary. What it takes to be considered great. There are people in this world who are afraid to be great! They're afraid to be champions only because they are afraid of the work and commitment required to be in the champions' pantheon.

But not you! Now go out there and be champions!"

Be the best! It's who you are.

About the Author
Blair Singer

For nearly three decades, Blair Singer has empowered people around the world to go beyond their ordinary selves and reach peak performance. He has rightfully earned a worldwide reputation as an expert in sales, business and personal growth.

He is a facilitator of personal and organizational change, a trainer and a dynamic public speaker. Blair's approach is one of high energy, intense and precise personal development and inspiration. His unique ability to get entire groups of people and organizations to shake up the status quo, change behaviors and achieve peak performance levels, in a very short period of time, is due to his high-impact approach.

As one of Robert Kiyosaki's original Rich Dad Advisors, Blair imparts two of the most critical skills and elements for success in business (and in life): being able to sell your idea, dream or concept and building a great team to deliver it. His unique slant, however, is that the road to success is paved through personal development and knowing how to overcome the limitations and obstacles that arise both personally and within groups.

Blair is the author of three best-selling books. *SalesDogs — You Don't Have to be an Attack Dog to Explode your Income, The Team Code of Honor* (these are Rich Dad Advisor series books) and his latest book, *Little Voice Mastery: How to Win the War Between Your Ears in 30 seconds or Less – and Have an Extraordinary Life!* His work has led to the creation of several personal and professional development programs that Blair facilitates in cities around the world.

SalesDogs offers sales and communication methodologies that have helped tens of thousands of people worldwide increase their income. This unique process identifies and magnifies an individual's or team's natural strengths and converts them into results, personal satisfaction and increased income.

Blair has conducted thousands of public and private seminars with audiences ranging in size from three to three hundred to over 10,000. Blair's clients span twenty countries on five continents and range from Fortune 100 companies to small business owners, entrepreneurs and sales teams. Blair's programs touch hundreds of thousands of people globally each year. He applies the same tried-and-true principals that work for big corporations and successful entrepreneurs to the Business of Everyday Living, helping individuals and companies hungry for greater success.

His clients typically experience sales and income growth of 34% to 260% in a matter of a few short months. For more information on Blair Singer, visit www.BlairSinger.com.

How Functional
(or Dysfunctional)
is Your Team?

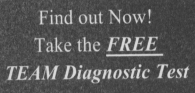

Find out Now!
Take the *FREE*
TEAM Diagnostic Test

www.blairsinger.com/
CodeofHonor

Ask yourself:

Are you operating
at peak efficiency?

Do your team members
trust each other?

Is everyone working
with purpose and
passion?

Other Books by
Blair Singer

Team Code of Honor
The Secrets of Champions in Business and in Life

Little Voice Mastery
How to Win the War Between Your Ears in 30 Seconds or Less —
and Have an Extraordinary Life!

References and Resources

For additional information, the following websites are suggested:

Books and Information for Investors and Entrepreneurs

www.BZKPress.com

Real Estate

www.Ken.Mcelroy.com

www.mccompanies.com

Asset Protection and LLC Formation

www.sutlaw.com

www.corporatedirect.com

Tax Planning

www.TaxFreeWealthBook.com

Sales Strategies

www.salesdogs.com

www.BlairSinger.com

The Rich Dad Company

www.RichDad.com

Is your "Little Voice" beating you up?

Telling you things like you are not good enough, smart enough, successful enough...enough of anything!

STOP THE BEATING <u>NOW</u>!

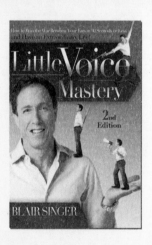

With *Little Voice Mastery*, you will learn to:

Maintain your power in any situation

Stop the debilitating chatter so you can attract what you want

End procrastination and resurrect level 10 confidence in any situation

Break through self-sabotaging habits

...in 30 seconds or less so you can eliminate hidden blockages and experience floods of income!

Accomplish & Earn More
in the next 6 Weeks

than you have in the
Past 6 Months

With the 6 Week "Little Voice" Mastery™ Mentoring Program

"In this program, I squashed the little voice in my head that said I wasn't good in sales and reset my commitment and confidence level. After the first 4 weeks of my program **I generated an additional $300,000 in revenue for my business**, over 6 times my original goal!" *Chris Baran, Fuel for Education*

"In the second week of the program my goal was to lose 14 pounds in weight in 4 remaining weeks. At the end of the program **I lost almost 30 pounds!** My husband and I have bought 3 rental properties and I've negotiated a contract for my business to work on an apprenticeship project with another large firm. So many wins to celebrate!" *Sara McManus, Business Owner and Property Investor*

You will receive weekly one-on-one sessions for 6 weeks taking you through a proven process that will help you:

- Become a bigger, **more powerful** YOU

- Have the confidence and capacity to **set goals** that are most important to you and reflect your true desires

- **Maintain accountability** to your goals and stay focused on what matters most

- **Eliminate procrastination**, limiting beliefs, and other self-sabotaging behaviors that hold you back from earning the income you deserve

- Manage the internal chatter – your "Little Voice" – so that you can **make decisions quickly** and confidently

- Experience the power of a daily gratitude process that will propel you towards your goals and **transform your life** and relationships

Blair Singer has personally created a training and certification program around his bestselling book "Little Voice" Mastery so only the most skilled mentors facilitate this program.

FREE

Schedule your **FREE 30-minute introductory** "Little Voice" Mastery mentoring session with a Certified **"Little Voice" Mastery** Mentor today.

www.LittleVoiceMentoring.com/book +1 (602) 224-7791

Experience...

The Ultimate Sales Mastery Program

Does $85,000 in 10 minutes sound like a lot of money to you? That's what participants in a recent program just accomplished!

Thousands of people have attended Blair Singer's **Ultimate Sales Mastery Program**. This program will help you:

★ Master the six steps of your selling cycle

★ Overcome any objection at any time

★ Work on YOUR business, YOUR products and YOURSELF

★ Maximize sales conversions

★ Turn an ordinary group into a championship sales team

RICH DAD ADVISORS

The Rich Dad Advisors series of books was created to deliver the how-to content to support Robert Kiyosaki's series of international bestsellers: *Rich Dad Poor Dad* and the Rich Dad series of books. In *Rich Dad Poor Dad*—the #1 Personal Finance Book of all Time—Robert presented the foundation for the Rich Dad principles and philosophies and set the stage for his context-changing messages that have changed the way the world thinks about money, business and investing.

The Rich Dad Advisors series of books has sold more than 2 million copies worldwide and BKZ Press, exclusive publisher of the Rich Dad Advisor series and the licensor of International Rights for the series, will be releasing several new titles that will expand both the scope and depth of the series.

Rich Dad Poor Dad represents the most successful book on personal finance in our generation. Over the last 15 years, its messages have inspired millions of people and impacted tens of millions of lives in over 100 countries around the world. The Rich Dad books have continued to stay on the international bestseller lists because their messages continue to resonate with readers of all ages. *Rich Dad Poor Dad* has succeeded in lifting the veil of confusion, fear, and frustration around money and replacing it with clarity, truth, and hope for every person who is willing to commit to the process of coming financially educated.

In order to make good on the promise of financial literacy and ultimate freedom, Robert Kiyosaki assembled his own team of personal and trusted advisors, proven experts in their respective fields, to deliver the only complete 'how-to' series of books and programs that takes the messages of Rich Dad to the streets of the world and gives each reader the step-by-step processes to achieve wealth and income in business, investing, and entrepreneurship.

BZK Press is driven by several of Kiyosaki's actual Advisors who have committed to take the messages of Rich Dad, convert them to practical applications and make sure those processes are put in the hands of those who seek financial literacy and financial freedom around the world. The series gives practical, proven processes to succeed in the areas of finance, tax, entrepreneurship, investing, property, debt, sales, wealth management and both business and personal development. Three of these trusted and accomplished Advisors—Blair Singer, Garrett Sutton, and Ken McElroy— are the driving forces behind BZK Press.

BZK Press is proud to assume the role of publisher of the Rich Dad Advisor series and perpetuate a series of books that has sold millions of copies worldwide and, more importantly, supported tens of millions in their journey toward financial freedom.

Best-Selling Books
in the Rich Dad Advisors Series

by Blair Singer

SalesDogs
You Don't Have to Be an Attack Dog to Explode Your Income

Team Code of Honor
The Secrets of Champions in Business and in Life

by Garrett Sutton, Esq.

Start Your Own Corporation
Why the Rich Own Their Own Companies and Everyone Else Works for Them

Writing Winning Business Plans
How to Prepare a Business Plan that Investors will Want to Read –
and Invest In

Buying and Selling a Business
How You Can Win in the Business Quadrant

The ABCs of Getting Out of Debt
Turn Bad Debt into Good Debt and Bad Credit into Good Credit

Run Your Own Corporation
How to Legally Operate and Properly Maintain Your Company
into the Future

by Ken McElroy

The ABCs of Real Estate Investing
The Secrets of Finding Hidden Profits Most Investors Miss

The ABCs of Property Management
What You Need to Know to Maximize Your Money Now

The Advanced Guide to Real Estate Investing
How to Identify the Hottest Markets and Secure the Best Deals

by Tom Wheelwright

Tax-Free Wealth
How to Build Massive Wealth by Permanently Lowering Your Taxes

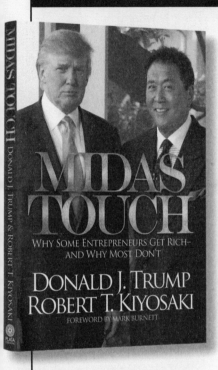

Notes